☑ W9-CCQ-118

BIBLE SURVIVAL

A Trivia Challenge for the Adventurous Soul

Tamela Hancock Murray

BARBOUR
PUBLISHING, INC.
Uhrichsville, Ohio

© 2001 by Barbour Publishing, Inc.

ISBN 1-58660-408-2

All rights reserved. No part of this publication may be
reproduced or transmitted in any form or by any means
without written permission of the publisher.

All Scripture quotations are taken from the King James
Version of the Bible.

Published by Barbour Publishing, Inc., P.O. Box 719,
Uhrichsville, Ohio 44683, http://www.barbourbooks.com

ecpa Member of the
Evangelical Christian
Publishers Association

Printed in the United States of America.

INTRODUCTION

Congratulations! You are a member of an elite group—one of those people chosen to participate in an incredible test of endurance and survival.

As a member of the "Christian" tribe, you'll be placed immediately into a hostile country full of danger and peril. Your challenge is to successfully navigate this alien territory, avoiding the many pitfalls, to arrive safely in the beautiful land of freedom and rest beyond.

Though the contest before you may seem impossible to win, recall the lessons you've studied in the approved survival manual—your Bible—as you forge ahead. This information, used properly, will guarantee you a successful journey.

You will meet some previous survivors along the way—individuals who have experienced many of the same challenges you have faced, and who will test your knowledge of the survival manual. Please understand that these fellow travelers cannot walk your path for you—they can only help to point you in the proper direction.

Now, the time has arrived—best wishes to you as you face the challenge of *Bible Survival*. Turn the page to meet your first fellow survivor.

SCORING

13–15 — Congratulations! Collect your prize
and move on to the next challenge.

10–12 — Brush up on the questions you missed
before moving on.

5–9 — Revisit the pertinent passages, as noted
in the answer key, before moving on.

0–4 — Take this opportunity to read and
study the story. Allow God to speak
to you through His Word.

Answers follow the
take-away point of each quiz.

QUIZ ONE

Good morning. I am the mother of
Samuel. On this island, as in life, you
will need both spiritual gifts and
tangible goods to survive. Because an
active prayer life is essential to
spiritual health, which is in turn first
and foremost to survival, this challenge focuses on my story. Godspeed!

My name is _____.

1. Hannah's story takes place in:
   a. 2 Samuel
   b. 1 Chronicles
   c. 1 Samuel
   d. 2 Chronicles

2. Hannah's husband, Elkanah, was a native of where?

3. When she discovered Hannah was barren, Elkanah's second wife, Peninnah:
   a. sold Hannah two mandrakes to make her more fertile
   b. went to the temple and prayed along with Hannah
   c. made fun of Hannah
   d. shared her mandrakes with Hannah

4. True or False: Elkanah's love for Hannah withered as her barrenness continued unabated.

5. When Eli saw Hannah praying, he thought she was _____.

6. When Hannah prayed to the Lord for a son, she promised Him that:
    a. no razor would touch his head
    b. she would name him "Samuel"
    c. her son would pray to the Lord each day
    d. Eli would be his mentor

7. True or False: Once Eli discovered the petition of Hannah's prayer, he told her to go in peace.

8. Hannah named her son Samuel because:
    a. she had promised the Lord she would
    b. she had asked the Lord for him
    c. she was told by God in a vision what to name him
    d. Eli said that Samuel should be the boy's name

9. Hannah presented Samuel to Eli soon after he was:
    a. circumcised
    b. bar mitzvahed
    c. weaned
    d. betrothed

10. The temple where Hannah took Samuel was located in _____.

11. Hannah said of Samuel, "I have lent him to the LORD." For how long?

12. True or False: After Samuel was gone, Hannah regretted her decision.

13. After Samuel's birth, Hannah had:
    a. no more children
    b. one other son
    c. three sons and two daughters
    d. one son and four daughters

14. Each year when he was a child, Hannah made Samuel a _____.

15. True or False: Eli didn't realize his sons were corrupt until after Samuel was grown.

Congratulations are in order
if you missed only one or two queries.
Otherwise, why don't you return to
1 Samuel and read about me?

That's all for me.
Your next inquisitor awaits.

Prayer is your hotline to the Lord.
Keep it open!

QUIZ ONE ANSWERS

My name is Hannah.

1. c. 1 Samuel
2. Hannah's husband, Elkanah, was a native of Ramathaim-zophim, of Mount Ephraim (1 Samuel 1:1).
3. c. made fun of Hannah (1 Samuel 1:6)
4. False (1 Samuel 1:5)
5. When Eli saw Hannah praying, he thought she was drunk (1 Samuel 1:13).
6. a. no razor would touch his head (1 Samuel 1:11). This meant he would be a Nazarite.
7. True (1 Samuel 1:17)
8. b. she had asked the Lord for him (1 Samuel 1:20)
9. c. weaned (1 Samuel 1:22)
10. The temple where Hannah took Samuel was located in Shiloh (1 Samuel 1:24).
11. She lent him to the Lord for his entire life (1 Samuel 1:28).
12. False (1 Samuel 2:1–10)
13. c. three sons and two daughters (1 Samuel 2:21)
14. Each year when he was a child, Hannah made Samuel a coat (1 Samuel 2:19).
15. False (1 Samuel 2:22–26)

QUIZ TWO

Shalom. Surely you remember me. After all, an entire book of the Bible bears my name. As you know from my story, survival can be tough, especially when you're faced with the unexpected.

If you can answer ten or more of the following questions, I will reward you with a salve that will keep you physically healthy while you're here. If only I'd had a salve for those awful boils!

Whether or not you spend your life in spiritual health depends on you—and your relationship with God. But more about that later. Let the second challenge begin!

My name is _____.

1. When Job was tested, how many sons and daughters did he have?

2. True or False: Job was so concerned about sin that he made sacrifices to the Lord on behalf of his sons, lest they had unintentionally sinned.

3. Why did Satan say that Job had been faithful to God?

4. Where had Satan been before he approached God?

5. The oxen and donkeys and all but one servant tending them were slaughtered by:
   a. Egyptians
   b. Assyrians
   c. Chaldeans
   d. Sabeans

6. The sheep and all but one of the servants tending them were destroyed by:
   a. a pack of wolves
   b. fire falling from heaven
   c. Chaldeans
   d. a flood

7. The camels and all but one servant were killed by whom?

8. Job's children were killed by:
   a. Assyrians
   b. fire
   c. wind
   d. hail

9. True or False: Job's children were still small when they were mortally wounded.

10. True or False: Job shaved his head when he found out about his losses.

11. Job said, "_____ came I out of my mother's womb, and _____ shall I return thither: the LORD gave, and the LORD hath taken away; blessed be the name of the LORD."

12. When Satan placed boils on him, Job scratched them with:
    a. broken pottery
    b. his fingernails
    c. the dull edge of a knife
    d. the tip of a stick

13. How many friends arrived to comfort Job?

14. What were their names?

15. True or False: Job's friends didn't speak to him for seven days and seven nights.

~

So how did you fare on my quiz? If you were unable to answer three or more questions, I suggest you go back and review my story. If you missed only one or two questions, congratulations! You earned the salve.

I, too, passed the most important test of my life after God agreed to let Satan tempt me. Though it wasn't easy, my perseverance was worth it all. After I suffered, God rewarded me with even more property. He blessed me with children who were more beautiful than any others around. I lived to be a very old man.

Have you ever wanted to blame God for your trials? If so, study my book of the Bible. It is my hope you will gather strength from my story. Remember that everyone is tempted. With God's help, temptation can be overcome.

Behold! Beyond the patch of palm trees
to the east, another man of the Bible
awaits. I bid you farewell.

Remember:
Do not be discouraged in times of trial.

BLESSED ARE

they which are persecuted
for righteousness' sake:
for theirs is the kingdom of heaven.
MATTHEW 5:10

QUIZ TWO ANSWERS

I am Job.

1. He had ten children—seven sons and three daughters (Job 1:2).
2. True (Job 1:5)
3. Satan claimed Job had been faithful only because the Lord had blessed him—because he had never been tested (Job 1:10–11).
4. Satan had been roaming to and fro upon the earth (Job 1:7).
5. d. Sabeans (Job 1:15)
6. b. fire falling from heaven (Job 1:16)
7. The camels and servants were destroyed by Chaldeans (Job 1:17).
8. c. wind (Job 1:19)
9. False (Job 1:4, 13)
10. True (Job 1:20)
11. Naked, naked (Job 1:21)
12. a. broken pottery (Job 2:8)
13. Three friends came to comfort him (Job 2:11).
14. Eliphaz, Bildad, and Zophar (Job 2:11).
15. True (Job 2:13)

QUIZ THREE

You will find my story in the Old Testament, which records the physical and spiritual path of my life. My treacherous ways set into motion a string of events. I fled my home, married sisters, wrestled an angel, and finally reconciled with my family and with God. How much of my story do you remember? If you can answer the questions on my test, I will reward you with a map of the island. How you navigate your spiritual life depends on your relationship with God.

I am _____.

1. The Bible says that Esau sold Jacob his birthright because he thought:
   a. Jacob was entitled to it
   b. he would die from hunger and would have no use for it
   c. Isaac favored Jacob and would deny the birthright to Esau
   d. Jacob would eventually return his rights to him

2. What did Jacob wear to make his father, whose eyes were dim with age, think he was hairy like Esau?

3. After Jacob stole Esau's birthright and blessing, his father told Jacob to go to the house of his uncle _____.

4. "And he dreamed, and behold a _____ set up on the earth, and the top of it reached to heaven: and behold the angels of God ascending and descending on it."

5. What was the name of Laban's daughter, whom Jacob loved best?
   a. Rachel
   c. Rebekah
   b. Leah
   d. Sarai

6. "And Jacob served _____ years for Rachel; and they seemed unto him but a few days, for the love he had to her."

7. After many years, Jacob left Laban's house. Why?

8. True or False: Jacob tried to flee Laban's house in secret.

9. True or False: When Jacob left Laban, as part of their covenant, Laban made Jacob promise not to take any more wives.

10. God promised Jacob that:
    a. he would be the father of kings
    b. all who hated him would be cursed
    c. he would have seven hundred wives
    d. he would be greater than Abraham

11. True or False: Jacob was renamed Israel.

12. Jacob's favorite son was Joseph because Joseph was:
    a. comely
    b. the eldest
    c. Rachel's son
    d. the son of his old age

13. After Joseph disappeared, Jacob didn't see him again until Joseph was:
    a. living in Egypt
    b. the father of two sons
    c. a member of Pharoah's royal court
    d. all of the above

14. True or False: Jacob's sons started the twelve tribes of Egypt.

15. True or False: After Jacob died, the Egyptians mourned him for seventy days.

~

If you answered at least thirteen questions correctly, you won a map of the island.

As you learned, I began life thinking treachery was the way to get what I wanted. But God protects His servants in spite of themselves.

God disciplined me, and believe me, that

22

was no fun! First, He allowed me to be the victim of deception. He wrestled with me in the desert. And He allowed me to live in fear of my brother. Thankfully, Esau proved himself to be a bigger man than I. My brother forgave me.

After my trials, I emerged victorious and spiritually mature. In hindsight, I'm grateful for His discipline.

Behold! I see someone I recognize. I wish you well on the next test.

Think about His will for your life.

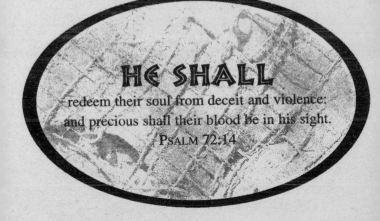

HE SHALL
redeem their soul from deceit and violence:
and precious shall their blood be in his sight.
PSALM 72:14

QUIZ THREE ANSWERS

I am Jacob.

1. b. he would die from hunger and would have no use for it (Genesis 25:32)
2. The skins of goat kids (Genesis 27:16)
3. Laban (Genesis 28:1–2)
4. ladder (Genesis 28:12)
5. a. Rachel (Genesis 29:18)
6. seven (Genesis 29:20)
7. "And Jacob beheld the countenance of Laban, and, behold, it was not toward him as before. And the LORD said unto Jacob, Return unto the land of thy fathers, and to thy kindred; and I will be with thee" (Genesis 31:2–3).
8. True (Genesis 31:20)
9. True (Genesis 31:50)
10. a. he would be the father of kings (Genesis 35:11–12)
11. True (Genesis 32:27–28, 35:9–10)
12. d. the son of his old age (Genesis 37:3)
13. d. all of the above (Genesis 37:28; 48:11–13; 47:1–2)
14. True (Genesis 49:28)
15. True (Genesis 50:1–3)

QUIZ FOUR

How lovely to see you! I've been told you've already earned the gift of prayer, a salve against physical afflictions, and a map. Yet whether you are facing challenges on this island or in life, you will be power less without love.

The elder of two sisters, I was given in marriage to a man who loved my sister more than he loved me. When God saw this, He remembered me by allowing me to bear many children. Now if you remember my story, you will be reminded of the importance of love.

I am _____.

1. Leah's story is recorded in what book of the Bible?

2. Leah's sister was named
   _____.

3. Leah is described as:
   a. homely
   b. comely
   c. tender-eyed
   d. robust

4. How long did Jacob work for Laban to earn Rachel's hand in marriage?

5. Can you name Leah's handmaid?

6. Through trickery, Laban forced Jacob to marry Leah before he married Rachel. Why?

7. How long did Jacob have to wait for Rachel after he wed Leah?
   a. another seven years
   b. one week
   c. one month
   d. until Leah conceived their first child

8. True or False: Once Jacob married Leah, he loved her as much as he loved Rachel.

9. "And when the_____ saw that Leah was hated, he opened her womb: but Rachel was barren."

10. How many sons did Leah bear before Rachel gave her handmaid to Jacob?

11. True or False: Leah's handmaid also bore Jacob two sons.

12. The fertility root mentioned in the story is:
    a. sassafras
    b. tapioca
    c. turnip
    d. mandrake

13. How many children did Leah bear?

14. True or False: Rachel, Leah, and their hand-maids Zilpah and Bilhah were the mothers of the twelve tribes of Israel.

15. True or False: Leah was buried with Jacob in Canaan.

Did my story help you remember the power of God's love? Although the world may not seem fair at times, His love abides.

In the distance
I see another woman of faith.
I leave you now to meet her.

God remembers the unloved.

QUIZ FOUR ANSWERS

I am Leah.

1. Genesis.
2. Rachel (Genesis 29:16)
3. c. tender-eyed (Genesis 29:17)
4. Seven years (Genesis 29:18)
5. Zilpah (Genesis 29:24)
6. "And Laban said, It must not be so done in our country, to give the younger before the firstborn" (Genesis 29:26).
7. b. one week (Genesis 29:27–28)
8. False (Genesis 29:30)
9. LORD (Genesis 29:31)
10. Four—Reuben, Simeon, Levi, and Judah (Genesis 29:32–35)
11. True (Genesis 30:9–13)
12. d. mandrake (Genesis 30:14)
13. Seven (Genesis 30:17–21)
14. True. Leah bore the six sons noted above. Rachel bore Joseph and Benjamin. Zilpah bore Gad and Asher. Bilhah bore Dan and Naphtali (Genesis 29:31–30:24 and Genesis 35:18).
15. True (Genesis 49:30–31)

QUIZ FIVE

I've been waiting for you. Not patiently, however. Patience was never my virtue. Over a period of many years, God taught me that waiting for His timing is best. Yet because I was impatient, my husband's seed spawned two nations.

I know you have already traveled a long way over the island without anything in which to carry your supplies. Demonstrate that you remember what the Bible says about me, and I'll grant you a bag made of camel skin.

I am _____.

1. What was Sarah called before she was renamed?

2. Impatient as she waited for a child, Sarah took matters into her own hands. How?

3. Hagar was:
    a. a handmaid
    b. an Egyptian
    c. the mother of Ishmael as a result of Sarah's decision
    d. all of the above

4. "But my covenant will I establish with _____, which Sarah shall bear unto thee at this set time in the next year."

5. Sarah was promised a son by:
    a. one angel
    b. Abraham
    c. Hagar
    d. three angels

6. What did Sarah do when she heard the news of the promise?

7. Why did she do this?

8. True or False: When Abraham told Abimelech that Sarah was his sister, he spoke the truth.

9. The Bible says that Sarah sent Hagar away because:
   a. Abraham had fallen in love with her
   b. she didn't want Isaac to share his inheritance with Ishmael
   c. Isaac was growing too fond of Hagar
   d. all of the above

10. Did the Lord tell Abraham to let Sarah send Hagar away?

11. Why or why not?

12. Sarah died in:
    a. Egypt
    b. the wilderness
    c. Israel
    d. Canaan

13. How old was she when she died?

14. What site did Abraham purchase as a family burial place?

15. Sarah, Abraham, Isaac, Rebekah, Leah, and Jacob were buried together. What family member is missing?

~

Congratulations! You have won the camel skin bag. You must travel on, but I shall remain here, awaiting word from the Lord as to what I should do. Finally, I have been blessed with the gift of patience. A good thing, too. I'm not as young as I once was, and I no longer move so swiftly.

When was the last time you were impatient for an answer from God? When He gave you an answer, how could you see that His timing was perfect?

I spy a flash of color.
The wearer of the coat is still a ways
from us, but he's certainly noticeable in
such a vibrant coat! Perhaps you should
go to him and find out who he is.

Wait upon the Lord's timing.

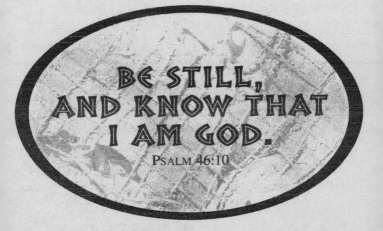

BE STILL,
AND KNOW THAT
I AM GOD.
PSALM 46:10

QUIZ FIVE ANSWERS

I am Sarah.

1. Sarai (Genesis 11:29)
2. She gave her handmaiden, Hagar, to her husband as a wife (Genesis 16:1–2).
3. d. all of the above (Genesis 16:1, 11)
4. Isaac (Genesis 17:21)
5. d. three angels (Genesis 18:2, 10)
6. She laughed (Genesis 18:12).
7. Under normal circumstances, she would have been too old to have children (Genesis 18:12).
8. True (Genesis 20:12). For the complete story about this deception and how God intervened, read Genesis 20.
9. b. she didn't want Isaac to share his inheritance with Ishmael (Genesis 21:10)
10. Yes (Genesis 21:12)
11. He told Abraham to listen to Sarah because Isaac would be his seed (Genesis 21:12).
12. d. Canaan (Genesis 23:2)
13. She was 127 years old (Genesis 23:1).
14. The cave of Machpelah (Genesis 23:19)
15. Rachel (Genesis 35:19)

QUIZ SIX

Good day to you. Do you remember me? When my jealous brothers sold me into slavery, they never dreamed that one day I would save their lives. If you can show me how much you know, a cup from which to drink— much like the one I slipped into Benjamin's bag—will be your reward.

I am _____.

1. Joseph's father was:
    a. Abraham
    b. Isaac
    c. Jacob
    d. Noah

2. What colorful garment did Joseph's father make for him?

3. Joseph dreamed:
    a. there would be famine
    b. he would be sold into slavery
    c. he would reign over his whole family
    d. he would be a slave to his brothers

4. Which brother thwarted the other brothers' plan to kill Joseph?

5. The brothers made their father believe that Joseph:
    a. was sold to Ishmaelites
    b. was sold to Egyptians
    c. ran away from home
    d. had been killed by a wild beast

6. True or False: Joseph was cast into prison based on the false testimony of Potiphar's wife.

7. True or False: Joseph gained favor with Pharaoh by interpreting his dreams.

8. What was God telling Pharaoh?

9. Joseph was eventually made ruler of what country?

10. True or False: Because of Joseph, his country had plenty to eat in time of famine.

11. After almost thirty years had passed, why did Joseph's brothers come to see him?

12. Did Joseph's brothers recognize Joseph when they saw him again?

13. True or False: Joseph couldn't reunite with his father because Jacob had died.

14. When Joseph saw his brothers, he:
    a. made fun of them for not taking his
       dream seriously
    b. slapped them for selling him into
       slavery
    c. thanked Reuben for saving his life
    d. provided for all of his brothers

15. True or False: Joseph was buried in Egypt,
    where he died at age 110.

I was a proud youth, but God humbled me when
I was thrown into prison through no fault of my
own. Likewise, He gave me the gift of interpreting dreams, which was part of His plan to raise
me into power so I could save the lives of many.

Please, take the cup. You earned it.

Has false pride ever stood in the way of your
faith walk? How did you overcome it? What did
a change in attitude bring?

Behold, I see a woman who
will stoop to deception for her favorite
son. I shall depart from you now so you
can learn about her. Godspeed.

Pride is humbled,
but God can mold
the repentant into greatness.

PRIDE GOETH
before destruction,
and an haughty spirit before a fall.
PROVERBS 16:18

QUIZ SIX ANSWERS

My name is Joseph.

1. c. Jacob (Genesis 37:2)
2. A coat of many colors (Genesis 37:3)
3. c. he would reign over his whole family (Genesis 37:5–7)
4. Reuben (Genesis 37:22)
5. d. had been killed by a wild beast (Genesis 37:31–36)
6. True (Genesis 39:7–23)
7. True (Genesis 41:14–44)
8. God was saying that seven years of plenty would be followed by seven years of famine (Genesis 41:25–32).
9. Egypt (Genesis 41:41)
10. True (Genesis 41:54)
11. They wanted to buy food (Genesis 42:3).
12. No (Genesis 42:8). Only later did Joseph reveal himself.
13. False (Genesis 46:29)
14. d. provided for all of his brothers (Genesis 47:11–12)
15. True (Genesis 50:26)

QUIZ SEVEN

Good morning. You were lucky to find me here at the well. As my story shows, survival can mean taking risks. But there's a difference between bravery and foolhardiness, and visiting a foreign island without water is foolhardy. Not to worry. I'm sure you'll be able to answer thirteen or more questions in my test. Once you do, you can have all the water you'll need for the rest of your stay.

By the way, how do you like my new gold earring and bracelets?

My name is _____.

1. Rebekah's story can be found in:
   a. Genesis
   b. Exodus
   c. 1 Kings
   d. Ruth

2. Who was Isaac's father, the man who was to become Rebekah's father-in-law?

3. Rebekah was from:
   a. Canaan
   b. Egypt
   c. Byzantium
   d. Mesopotamia

4. Why did Isaac's father send his servant to this particular place to find a wife for his son?

5. What did the servant do as he waited for the right woman to approach him at the well?

6. The servant gave Rebekah an earring and two bracelets for:
   a. her great beauty
   b. giving him a drink and watering his camels
   c. sharing the news that Jesus is the Messiah
   d. a night's lodging at the home of her father

7. Rebekah's father, Bethuel, and her brother, Laban, said they agreed that Rebekah could leave home to marry Isaac because:
    a. they knew and liked Abraham
    b. the servant had given her jewelry
    c. in addition to the jewelry, Abraham's servant gave them two hundred goats
    d. the Lord had spoken

8. True or False: Once Bethuel and Laban made their decision, Rebekah had no say in the matter.

9. Isaac was comforted in his new marriage to Rebekah after the death of his:
    a. mother   c. father
    b. brother   d. first wife

10. True or False: Within months after their marriage, Rebekah conceived twins.

11. True or False: After Rebekah bore the twins, the Bible mentions that she bore three more sons named Shem, Ham, and Japheth.

12. "And Isaac loved Esau, because he did eat of his venison: but Rebekah loved _____."

13. True or False: Rebekah gave Jacob the idea that he should deceive his father to steal Esau's blessing.

14. Once the plot succeeded, setting off Esau's ire, Rebekah told Isaac that Jacob should flee to her brother's home because:
    a. Laban could teach Jacob a trade
    b. Esau wanted to kill Jacob
    c. she didn't want Jacob to marry a local girl
    d. Jacob could carry food to Laban since her homeland was experiencing famine

15. Genesis 49:31 says: "There they buried Abraham and Sarah his wife; there they buried Isaac and Rebekah his wife; and there I buried Leah." Who is speaking?

❧

Welcome back. I trust you were able to answer at least thirteen questions easily. Please, take all the water you and your animals require.

As you learned, following the Lord's will

often takes courage. That evening when I met Abraham's servant at the well, I never expected the Lord's plan for my life to unfold. And even though my father and brother approved, leaving my family to marry a stranger in a foreign land was an act of courage.

Has your faith ever taken you down a road you didn't expect? How did the Lord ultimately reward your perseverance?

I see in the distance a woman of ill repute. Let me exit now, as I do not wish to speak to her.

Survival may mean taking risks.

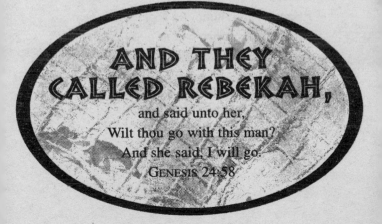

AND THEY CALLED REBEKAH, and said unto her, Wilt thou go with this man? And she said, I will go.
GENESIS 24:58

QUIZ SEVEN ANSWERS

My name is Rebekah.

1. a. Genesis
2. Abraham (Genesis 24:1)
3. d. Mesopotamia (Genesis 24:10)
4. Abraham chose the home of his kindred (Genesis 24:7).
5. He prayed (Genesis 24:12–14).
6. b. giving him a drink and watering his camels (Genesis 24:17–23)
7. d. the Lord had spoken. (Genesis 24:50–51)
8. False (Genesis 24:58)
9. a. mother (Genesis 24:67)
10. False (Genesis 25:21)
11. False. Shem, Ham, and Japheth were Noah's sons (Genesis 5:32).
12. Jacob (Genesis 25:28)
13. True (Genesis 27:6–10)
14. c. she didn't want Jacob to marry a local girl (Genesis 27:46)
15. Jacob (Genesis 49:33)

QUIZ EIGHT

Perhaps you think you caught me by
surprise, but I spied you long ago.
Are you ready to take my challenge?
If you pass, you will be awarded
scarlet thread. Of course it is valuable.
A prophet told me people in the future
will horde paper clips, rubber bands,
and wads of aluminum foil. I'm not
certain what those things are, but surely
thread is just as worthy. Best wishes!

My name is _____.

1. True or False: Although Rahab's story is recorded in the Old Testament, she is mentioned at least twice in the New Testament.

2. What book of the Bible records Rahab's story?

3. According to the Bible, Rahab was a:
    a. prostitute
    b. widow
    c. virgin
    d. priestess

4. The spies were sent out of:
    a. Canaan
    b. Egypt
    c. Shittim
    d. Bethlehem

5. Who sent the spies?

6. True or False: The king of Jericho soon discovered that Rahab was hiding spies.

7. The king decided to:
    a. kill Rahab as a traitor
    b. kill Rahab and the spies
    c. ask Rahab to turn in the spies
    d. bribe Rahab with thirty talents to turn in the spies

8. True or False: Rahab lied to the king about the spies' whereabouts.

9. Rahab hid the spies:
    a. on the roof of her house
    b. at the house of a friend
    c. in the cellar of her house
    d. with a priest at the temple

10. Why did Rahab help the spies?

11. In return for her help, what did the spies promise Rahab?

12. Rahab was to mark her house with a _____ thread.

13. True or False: The spies broke their word to Rahab because Joshua opposed the deal they made with her.

14. True or False: Rahab is included in Jesus' lineage.

15. Not all the women in Jesus' line lived impeccable lives. Can you name the adulteress who eventually wed King David and bore Solomon?

Were you able to answer at least thirteen questions? Excellent. Then you understand from my story that God can use anyone to do His will. I did not live a perfect life, but through my faith, God was able to use me to carry out His plan.

Have you ever seen God use a questionable person to carry out His will? How did that affect your faith walk?

Behold! I smell a savory stew.
Do you smell the delicious odor?
Let's see who is cooking it now.

Do you sometimes doubt God can use you
because of your imperfections?
Pray about it.

AND JOSHUA
saved Rahab the harlot alive,
and her father's household, and all that she had;
and she dwelleth in Israel even unto this day;
because she hid the messengers,
which Joshua sent to spy out Jericho.
JOSHUA 6:25

QUIZ EIGHT ANSWERS

My name is Rahab.

1. True (Hebrews 11:31; James 2:25)
2. Joshua
3. a. prostitute (Joshua 2:1)
4. c. Shittim (Joshua 2:1)
5. Joshua sent the spies (Joshua 2:1).
6. True (Joshua 2:2–3)
7. c. ask Rahab to turn in the spies
   (Joshua 2:3)
8. True (Joshua 2:5)
9. a. on the roof of her house (Joshua 2:6)
10. She helped them because she believed in
    the Lord. She had heard stories of the
    Lord's greatness and knew that the Lord
    had given the Israelites the land
    (Joshua 2:9).
11. They promised to spare her family when the
    city was attacked (Joshua 2:12–14).
12. scarlet (Joshua 2:18, 21)
13. False (Joshua 6:17, 22–23)
14. True (Matthew 1:5)
15. Bathsheba (Matthew 1:6; 2 Samuel 11:3)

QUIZ NINE

There you are. I've been waiting for you. How do you like the delicious smell that arises from my dish? I have prepared a savory stew. Care for a bowl? My price is not your birth-right—like my brother charged me—but simply proof you remember what the Bible says about my life.

My name is _____.

1. Where can you find Esau's story in the Bible?

2. Who was Esau's mother?

3. Esau liked to:
   - a. sail
   - b. fish
   - c. study the Torah
   - d. hunt

4. To whom did Esau sell his birthright?

5. True or False: When he took his first wife, Esau pleased his parents by choosing a godly woman who strengthened his faith in the one true God.

6. After Jacob stole Esau's blessing, Isaac blessed Esau by saying:
   - a. Esau would serve his brother, asserting his independence from time to time
   - b. God would grant him riches
   - c. Esau's faith would soon grow
   - d. Jacob would pay for his duplicity by serving him

7. True or False: Although at first Esau was

angry with Jacob for stealing his birthright and blessing, he did not let the sun set on his anger.

8. Who had the idea to send Jacob to his uncle?
   a. Isaac
   b. Rebekah
   c. Esau
   d. Jacob

9. What did Esau do when he saw that Jacob was obedient to Isaac by marrying women from their extended family?

10. How many men did Esau have with him when he reunited with Jacob?

11. True or False: As soon as Jacob saw Esau, he drew his sword.

12. When Esau saw Jacob, he:
   a. drew his sword
   b. ran toward him and kissed him
   c. instructed his men to kill Jacob
   d. demanded recompense for Jacob's deceit

13. Jacob called himself Esau's:
    a. servant
    b. master
    c. brother
    d. kinsman

14. What did Esau initially say about Jacob's gifts?

15. "So Esau returned that day on his way unto _____."

If you answered at least thirteen questions, then you have earned your bowl of stew. Enjoy!

All my life, it seemed as though I couldn't win. No matter what I did to please my parents, I couldn't earn their favor. This reminds me of how God works in our lives. No matter what we do, there's no way we can earn His favor.

But He does grant forgiveness. If we only ask, He grants us forgiveness freely. Likewise, I didn't want the gifts my brother presented me with upon our reconciliation. I freely forgave him for his treachery against me.

Do you have someone in your life you need to forgive? Pray about it.

Behold! A beautiful woman awaits with dessert. I wonder what questions she will pose to you?

Those who forgive live in the light of forgiveness.

FORGIVE, AND YE SHALL BE FORGIVEN.

LUKE 6:37

QUIZ NINE ANSWERS

My name is Esau.

1. Genesis, chapters 25–36
2. Rebekah, Isaac's wife (Genesis 25:20–26)
3. d. hunt (Genesis 25:27)
4. His brother Jacob (Genesis 25:31–32)
5. False (Genesis 26:34–35)
6. a. Esau would serve his brother, asserting his independence from time to time (Genesis 27:40).
7. False: Esau planned to kill Jacob soon after their father died (Genesis 27:41).
8. b. Rebekah (Genesis 27:42–43)
9. He married a descendent of Ishmael (Genesis 28:9).
10. Four hundred (Genesis 33:1)
11. False (Genesis 33:3)
12. b. ran toward him and kissed him (Genesis 33:4)
13. a. servant (Genesis 33:5). He also called him "my lord" (Genesis 33:8, 14–15).
14. He didn't want to accept them, protesting he had enough (Genesis 33:9).
15. Seir (Genesis 33:16)

QUIZ TEN

Greetings. It's been hours since you last ate. By now you must be hungry. In my story, two banquets were involved in my plan to save my people. If you can answer ten of the following questions, your reward will be a pint of dates, much like those served at my table.

My name is _____.

1. Esther's husband, Ahasuerus (also known as Xerxes), ruled 127 provinces from:
   a. India to Ethiopia
   b. Egypt to Israel
   c. Canaan to Egypt
   d. Egypt to Ethiopia

2. True or False: Queen Vashti willingly joined the king's feast so he could show her beauty to everyone present.

3. Mordecai was Esther's:
   a. cousin
   b. uncle
   c. father
   d. friend

4. Even after she had been living in the women's house of the king's palace for some time, why hadn't Esther revealed that she was Jewish?

5. Before a night with the king, the women were purified for:
   a. one month
   b. three days
   c. one year
   d. seven days

6. After Esther became queen, Mordecai found favor by:
   a. doubling the grapes produced by the king's vineyards
   b. foiling an assassination attempt on a provincial governor
   c. foiling an assassination attempt on the king
   d. storing enough grain to take the provinces through a seven-year famine

7. Why did Mordecai refuse to bow to Haman?

8. True or False: A kind man, Haman understood and respected Mordecai's decision not to bow to him.

9. True or False: Queen Esther discovered something was wrong when her maids told her that Mordecai was grieving.

10. After Esther agreed to speak to the king, she told Mordecai to tell her people to:
    a. tear their clothes
    b. spread sheep's blood on their doors
    c. fast for three days
    d. not to worry

11. Why was Esther's act of speaking to the king so courageous?

12. True or False: Haman was worried about attending Esther's banquets.

13. Haman was so angry that Mordecai continued to refuse to bow to him that he:
    a. hastened to carry out his plot
    b. had the king declare war on the nation of Israel
    c. immediately confiscated the Jews' land
    d. had a hanging gallows built

14. True or False: Haman was punished, but his ten sons were spared.

15. What remembrance was begun to celebrate Queen Esther and the deliverance of the Jews?

Because I risked my own life to speak to my husband, I saved my people from certain destruction. When the king heard the details of Haman's plot, he authorized the Jews to resist without interference. God was with them, and they were victorious. For all of the details, read the book of the Bible that bears my name.

I hope you will never be tested in your quest for survival as I was. However, I wish you courage if you are. Farewell.

Survival means overcoming fear.

FEAR NOT, LITTLE FLOCK;
for it is your Father's good pleasure to give you the kingdom.
LUKE 12:32

QUIZ TEN ANSWERS

My name is Esther.

1. a. India to Ethiopia (Esther 1:1)
2. False (Esther 1:12)
3. a. cousin (Esther 2:5–7). However, he thought of the orphaned Esther as his daughter.
4. Mordecai told her not to reveal her heritage (Esther 2:20). He had also told her not to reveal her heritage earlier (Esther 2:10).
5. c. one year (Esther 2:12–14)
6. c. foiling an assassination attempt on the king (Esther 2:21–23)
7. Mordecai refused because he was Jewish (Esther 3:4).
8. False (Esther 3:5–6)
9. True (Esther 4:1–7)
10. c. fast for three days (Esther 4:16)
11. Asking to speak to the king could have resulted in her death (Esther 4:11).
12. False (Esther 5:12)
13. d. had a hanging gallows built (Esther 5:14)
14. False (Esther 9:13–14)
15. Purim (Esther 9:31)

QUIZ ELEVEN

Greetings—I know what you're thinking. Why is this man wearing a loin cloth, and why is he so unkempt?

Queen Esther's dates will keep you going for awhile, but if you can demonstrate that you know about me, I'll teach you where to find locusts and wild honey. Don't cringe. They're not so bad. Kind of crunchy.

Besides, the food we eat is not important. What really matters is the Son of God! But since God the Father knows our bodies need food to survive, we'll move on to the test.

My name is_____.

1. True or False: John the Baptist wrote the Gospel of John.

2. John's birth was predicted in:
   - a. Matthew
   - b. Mark
   - c. Luke
   - d. all of the above

3. Can you give the name of John's mother?*

4. John's father was a:
   - a. priest
   - b. merchant
   - c. carpenter
   - d. shepherd

5. True or False: The angel of the Lord identified himself by name to Zacharias, John's father.

6. What was Zacharias doing when the angel visited him?
   - a. burning incense in the temple
   - b. haggling over the price of an alabaster bottle filled with perfume
   - c. making a table
   - d. tending his flock

7. Those who circumcised John called the new baby by what name?

8. After John's father wrote that the baby was to be named John, he:
   a. glowed from being in the presence of God
   b. lost his sight
   c. regained his power of speech
   d. was able to walk again

9. John the Baptist preached in the wilderness located in _____.

10. John said, "Repent ye, for:
    a. the truth shall set you free"
    b. the son of God is born"
    c. the kingdom of heaven is at hand"
    d. thou shall go and sin no more"

11. John's life was spoken of by the prophet:
    a. Isaiah   c. Elisha
    b. Elijah   d. Nathan

12. Whose shoes did John say he was not worthy to bear?

13. John said Jesus would baptize with the Holy Ghost and with:
    a. wine
    b. fire
    c. ashes
    d. water

14. True or False: John the Baptist begged Jesus for the privilege of baptizing Him since He is the Son of God.

15. After Jesus was baptized, a voice from heaven said, "This is my beloved Son, in whom I am well _____."

～

I see you have returned. I trust you were able to answer at least thirteen questions.

As you remember, there were some powerful people who didn't like what I had to say. Yet I spoke the truth. I paid for my honesty with my life.

Don't lose your savor. Return each day to the Word of God. Ask Him to renew you with the Holy Spirit. Many souls need salvation in your day, as did many in mine. Today's followers of Christ are His ambassadors for this generation.

Salt the earth freely with the Word of the Lord.

I see someone else waiting.
Grace to you.

Remember:
We are commanded to speak the truth,
regardless of the cost.

YE ARE THE

salt of the earth: but if the salt have lost his savour, wherewith shall it be salted? it is thenceforth good for nothing, but to be cast out, and to be trodden under foot of men.

MATTHEW 5:13

QUIZ ELEVEN ANSWERS

My name is John the Baptist.

1. False. The Gospel of John is attributed to the apostle John, the son of Zebedee.
2. c. Luke (1:13–19)
3. Elisabeth (Luke 1:13)
4. a. priest (Luke 1:5)
5. True (Luke 1:19)
6. a. burning incense in the temple (Luke 1:9–12)
7. Zacharias (Luke 1:59)
8. c. regained his power of speech (Luke 1:63–64)
9. Judea (Matthew 3:1)
10. c. the kingdom of heaven is at hand (Matthew 3:2)
11. a. Isaiah (Matthew 3:3)
12. Jesus' (Matthew 3:11)
13. b. fire (Matthew 3:11)
14. False (Matthew 3:13–15)
15. pleased (Matthew 3:17)

QUIZ TWELVE

There you are! Since you've gotten this far, you must have learned how to gather food. Now you'll need shelter. This island can get pretty unpleasant without somewhere to keep out of the rain. If there's anything I know how to survive, it's flooding. Prove yourself to me, and I'll provide you with enough boards to build a small shelter.

I am _____.

1. Noah's story is recorded in the book of
   _____.

2. Noah's story begins in what chapter?

3. Can you name Noah's three sons?

4. What significant event concerning man's
   lifespan occurred during Noah's time?

5. "Noah found _____ in the eyes of the
   Lord."

6. God instructed Noah to make the ark:
   a. 300 cubits long, 50 cubits wide,
       and 30 cubits high
   b. 400 cubits long, 50 cubits wide,
       and 60 cubits high
   c. 300 cubits long, 50 cubits wide,
       and 60 cubits high
   d. 400 cubits long, 30 cubits wide,
       and 30 cubits high

7. True or False: All the animals went to the
   ark two by two.

8. Once the flooding was over, the mountain tops could first be seen after:
   a. twelve months
   b. two months
   c. five months
   d. ten months

9. Soon after Noah left the ark, he built:
   a. a temple
   b. a home out of driftwood
   c. an altar and sacrificed one of each clean beast
   d. an altar and sacrificed one lamb without blemish

10. True or False: The rainbow no longer represents God's promise not to flood the entire earth.

11. Which of Noah's sons is the father of Canaan?

12. After the flood, the Bible says that Noah:
    a. planted a vegetable garden
    b. planted a vineyard
    c. bred goats and sheep
    d. divided the land equally between his three sons

13. Noah cursed Canaan because:
    a. Ham had seen Noah naked and then told his brothers
    b. Ham worshiped a golden calf
    c. Ham was drunk on wine
    d. Ham had refused to take part in sacrificial ceremonies

14. When they learned about Ham's indiscretion, Shem and Japheth:
    a. covered their father without looking upon him
    b. destroyed the golden calf
    c. poured the rest of the wine onto the ground
    d. banished him from the family

15. How many years after the flood did Noah live?

Did you answer all the questions, or at least thirteen? Good. Then the boards are yours.

Praise God for His promise not to destroy the earth by a flood ever again.

Perhaps I appeared silly when I built a huge ark on dry land. By following God's will without question, my entire family was spared the death experienced by the rest of the world.

Have you ever felt doubtful, or even silly, when you followed God's will? How were you blessed by staying faithful to Him?

Behold, a carpenter approacheth.
I take leave of you now.

God keeps His promises.

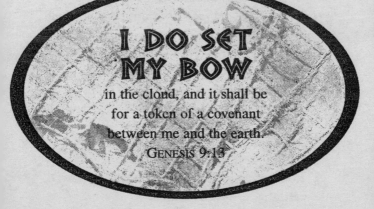

I DO SET MY BOW in the cloud, and it shall be for a token of a covenant between me and the earth.
GENESIS 9:13

QUIZ TWELVE ANSWERS

My name is Noah.

1. Noah's story is recorded in the book of Genesis.
2. Noah's story begins in Genesis, chapter 5, verse 29.
3. Noah's three sons were Shem, Ham, and Japheth (Genesis 5:32).
4. During Noah's time, the lifespan of humans was shortened to 120 years (Genesis 6:3).
5. "Noah found grace in the eyes of the Lord" (Genesis 6:8).
6. a. 300 cubits long, 50 cubits wide, and 30 cubits high (Genesis 6:15).
7. False (Genesis 7:2)
8. d. ten months (Genesis 8:5)
9. c. an altar and sacrificed one of each clean beast (Genesis 8:20)
10. False (Genesis 9:12–13)
11. Ham is the father of Canaan (Genesis 9:18).
12. b. planted a vineyard (Genesis 9:20)
13. a. Ham had seen Noah naked and then told his brothers (Genesis 9:22–25)
14. a. covered their father without looking upon him (Genesis 9:23)
15. Noah lived 350 years after the flood (Genesis 9:28).

QUIZ THIRTEEN

Greetings! I'm not surprised to see you. Putting together boards with pitch is a bit tricky, isn't it? Never was any good at it myself. As a carpenter, I prefer a hammer and wooden nails. I'll give you a hammer and nails in abundance if you pass my test.

I am _____.

1. True or False: Joseph, the earthly father of Jesus, is mentioned in Luke.

2. True or False: Joseph believed Mary when she told him she was to give birth to God's Son.

3. Who told Joseph the name of Mary's baby?

4. Joseph discovered Jesus' purpose on earth:
   a. when the king threatened to kill the infant Jesus
   b. before Jesus was born
   c. when Jesus performed His first miracle at Cana
   d. the day Jesus was crucified

5. What does "Immanuel" mean?

6. Bethlehem is the city of _____.

7. Why did Joseph go to Bethlehem for the census instead of registering in his hometown?

8. In the second appearance of the angel to Joseph, he was told:
   a. not to put Mary away
   b. to go to Egypt
   c. he could safely return home with his family
   d. to flee to Nazareth

9. True or False: Herod told the wise men he wanted to worship the infant Jesus.

10. Herod sent what people to find Jesus?

11. After they saw Jesus, the wise men knew that they shouldn't return to Herod because of:
    a. a dream
    b. the alignment of the stars
    c. the warning of a shepherd
    d. the warning of a member of Herod's royal court

12. An angel appeared in a dream to Joseph while he was in Egypt and told him to take his family to Israel. What had happened?

13. Why did Joseph turn toward Galilee after entering Israel, despite God's instructions?

14. "And he came and dwelt in a city called _____: that it might be fulfilled which was spoken by the prophets, He shall be called a Nazarene."

15. True or False: Joseph's story is recorded in detail in the book of Mark.

If you passed my quiz, I am pleased to reward you with the hammer and nails. I am certain you will build a fine shelter. As you can see from my life, I had doubts about my betrothed, Mary. How thankful I am that God told me to stay with her. Had He not, I would not have enjoyed the privilege of nurturing Jesus as His earthly father.

One of the patriarchs is waiting to
give you the next test.
I bid you farewell.

Remember:
Follow God, even in doubt.

BUT WHILE

he thought on these things, behold,
the angel of the Lord appeared unto him in a
dream, saying, Joseph, thou son of David,
fear not to take unto thee Mary thy wife:
for that which is conceived
in her is of the Holy Ghost.

MATTHEW 1:20

QUIZ THIRTEEN ANSWERS

My name is Joseph.

1. True (Luke 1:27)
2. False (Matthew 1:18–21)
3. The Lord's angel told Joseph the name (Matthew 1:20–21).
4. b. before Jesus was born (Matthew 1:21)
5. "God with us" (Matthew 1:23)
6. David (Luke 2:4)
7. Joseph was required to go to Bethlehem, the city of David, because Joseph was of the line of David (Luke 2:4).
8. b. to go to Egypt (Matthew 2:13)
9. True (Matthew 2:8)
10. Herod sent the wise men to find Jesus (Matthew 2:7–8).
11. a. a dream (Matthew 2:12)
12. Herod had died (Matthew 2:19–20).
13. He left Israel for Galilee after he heard that Archelaus, Herod's son, reigned in Judea. Joseph was afraid (Matthew 2:22).
14. Nazareth (Matthew 2:23)
15. False. However, he is mentioned in Matthew, Luke, and John.

QUIZ FOURTEEN

Shalom. Let me guess. You want advice? Throughout my life, the people of Israel sought my advice.

Or perhaps you were drawn to the burning bush. It got my attention! Now that you have your shelter and know how to find food, you're probably wondering how to keep warm when the temperature drops at night. If you can answer at least thirteen of the following questions correctly, I'll provide you with a lit torch so you can enjoy the benefits of fire during the remainder of your stay.

I am _____.

1. What five books of the Bible did Moses write?

2. True or False: Moses' story begins in the book of Genesis.

3. Why did Pharaoh decree that all the Hebrew baby boys be killed?

4. Moses' basket floating in the river was found by:
   a. Pharaoh's servant
   b. Pharaoh's daughter
   c. Pharaoh
   d. Pharaoh's daughter's handmaiden

5. After he was grown, Moses fled Egypt because he:
   a. stole from the treasury
   b. was found to be a Hebrew
   c. killed an Egyptian for smiting a Hebrew
   d. killed a Hebrew for smiting a member of the royal court

6. When God spoke to Moses, what name did the LORD use for Himself?

7. When the Lord commissioned Moses to speak to Pharaoh about releasing His people, Moses said he was:
   a. not an eloquent speaker
   b. honored to be chosen
   c. not qualified since he wasn't a priest
   d. going to wait until after Passover

8. During the plagues, what remembrance was instituted that is still observed by the Jewish people today?

9. What sea was parted as the people exited?

10. After the Israelites complained that they had no meat after they left Egypt, God sent:
    a. doves
    b. quail
    c. salmon
    d. cattle

11. True or False: Manna is described in the Bible.

12. Why were judges appointed during the time Moses led the people?

13. True or False: The original stone tablets on which the Ten Commandments were written are thought to exist to this day, but archaeologists have been unable to find them.

14. After Moses became angry with the Israelites for disobeying God, he:
    a. refused to lead them any more
    b. interceded for them with God
    c. helped them rebuild their idol
    d. returned to Egypt

15. After Moses' death, who succeeded him?

Welcome back. If you answered the questions correctly, good for you. You have earned the lit torch. I'm sure your food will taste much better now that you can cook!

As you can see, I didn't want to follow God's calling for me. I tried to convince Him that I never could articulate His wishes to Pharaoh. But I wasn't going to get out of serving Him that easily. He made provision for me.

Have you ever tried to squirm out of a

difficult task that God wanted you to do? What happened? How did He provide so that you could serve His purpose?

I see the woman who
is to test you next.
I shall depart from you now.

The power of God is
with those who seek Him.

THY
RIGHT HAND,
O LORD, is become glorious in power:
thy right hand, O LORD,
hath dashed in pieces the enemy.
EXODUS 15:6

QUIZ FOURTEEN ANSWERS

I am Moses.

1. The Pentateuch—Genesis, Exodus, Leviticus, Numbers, Deuteronomy
2. False. His story begins in Exodus, beginning with his birth (Exodus 2).
3. Because he was afraid they would multiply and eventually join Egypt's enemies in war (Exodus 1:10).
4. b. Pharaoh's daughter (Exodus 2:5)
5. c. killed an Egyptian for smiting a Hebrew (Exodus 2:11–12 and 15)
6. I AM and/or I AM THAT I AM (Exodus 3:14)
7. a. not an eloquent speaker (Exodus 4:10)
8. Passover (Exodus 12:1–28)
9. the Red Sea (Exodus 13–18, 14:21–31)
10. b. quail (Exodus 16:12–13)
11. True (Exodus 16:31)
12. Moses was overwhelmed by the number of people who sought his advice and arbitration in disputes (Exodus 18:13–22).
13. False. Moses broke them in anger when the Israelites disobeyed God by making and worshiping a golden calf (Exodus 32:19).
14. b. interceded for them with God (Exodus 32:30–32)
15. Joshua, son of Nun (Deuteronomy 34:9)

QUIZ FIFTEEN

Good afternoon. Elijah told me I would see you. I understand that you've acquired fire, and now you desire oil for cooking. Of course I am willing to accommodate you. Please take the following test. Elijah hasn't told me whether or not you shall pass it. I have confidence you will!

I am _____.

1. The name of the widow who sustained Elijah:
   - a. was Miriam
   - b. was Mary
   - c. was Martha
   - d. is unknown

2. Where in the Bible do we find the widow's story?

3. True or False: Elijah met the woman by accident.

4. In what city did the woman live?

5. When he first saw her, the widow was:
   - a. gathering sticks
   - b. pressing olives for oil
   - c. grinding wheat
   - d. drawing water from the well

6. She was doing this so she could:
   - a. make bread for dinner
   - b. sell the oil for a pretty price at the market
   - c. bake unleavened bread for Passover
   - d. give drink to the goat that provided her with milk

7. Elijah asked her for:
    a. the fatted calf and a cask of ale
    b. bread and water
    c. lentil stew and bread
    d. wine and bread

8. The woman was reluctant to meet Elijah's request because:
    a. Elijah was known to overindulge and would eat all her food
    b. having a drunken man in her home would ruin her reputation
    c. Elijah was moody and might not like the dinner
    d. she had just enough flour and oil for one last meal before she starved

9. "For thus saith the LORD God of Israel, The barrel of meal shall not waste, neither shall the cruse of oil fail, until the day that the LORD sendeth _____ upon the earth."

10. Who fell ill and died after Elijah had resided with the woman for some time?

11. When this happened, why did the woman think Elijah had come to stay with her?

12. Elijah took the victim to:
    a. the Jordan River
    b. the loft where he was staying
    c. Jerusalem
    d. the nearest temple

13. "And he stretched himself upon the child
    _____ times, and cried unto the LORD,
    and said, O LORD my God, I pray thee, let
    this child's soul come into him again."

14. True or False: Elijah was unable to re-
    vive him.

15. After Elijah performed this miracle, what
    did the woman tell him she knew about him?

~

Did you answer thirteen questions correctly?
Congratulations! You have earned enough oil to
cook with during your stay on the island. Were
you worried you would not have enough food, or
any way to prepare it? As you can see, I was
worried about my food supply when Elijah
arrived. In fact, I was in the process of making

what I thought would be the last meal my son
and I would eat when Elijah assured me we
would have plenty of food until the next rain.
The Lord is good!

Have you ever been worried about having
enough of life's necessities? How did the Lord
provide for you?

I behold a tainted woman on the horizon.
Go to her, and learn your lesson well.

Be faithful to those who serve the Lord.
He will provide.

IF ANY MAN
SERVE ME,
let him follow me; and where I am,
there shall also my servant be:
if any man serve me,
him will my Father honour.
JOHN 12:26

QUIZ FIFTEEN ANSWERS

I am the widow who sustained Elijah, and/or the widow of Zarephath.

1. d. is unknown. (The Bible does not tell us.)
2. 1 Kings, chapter 17
3. False. The Lord told Elijah that the widow would sustain him (1 Kings 17:9).
4. Zarephath (1 Kings 17:9)
5. a. gathering sticks (1 Kings 17:10)
6. a. make bread for dinner (1 Kings 17:12)
7. b. bread and water (1 Kings 17:10–11)
8. d. she had just enough flour and oil for one last meal before she starved (1 Kings 17:12)
9. Rain (1 Kings 17:14)
10. The widow's son (1 Kings 17:17)
11. She thought he had come to rebuke her for her sin (1 Kings 17:18). No specific sin is mentioned.
12. b. the loft where he was staying (1 Kings 17:19)
13. Three (1 Kings 17:21)
14. False (1 Kings 17:23)
15. "And the woman said to Elijah, Now by this I know that thou art a man of God, and that the word of the LORD in thy mouth is truth" (1 Kings 17:24).

QUIZ SIXTEEN

I sinned by betraying my husband.
The religious leaders showed me no
mercy, but Jesus forgave me. So if
you have come here to judge me, I
suggest you exercise caution.

As you take the following quiz,
reflect on how His wisdom can
change your life, too. If you're profi-
cient in your answers, I'll share with
you an earthenware pan so that you
may cook over the fire.

I am _____.

1. True or False: The story of the adulteress appears in two Gospel accounts.

2. The event occurred in what geographic location?
   a. Mount Hermon
   b. the Garden of Gethsemane
   c. the Mount of Olives
   d. in an unspecified location

3. In what structure did the event occur?

4. The adulteress's accusers interrupted Jesus as He was:
   a. eating   c. teaching
   b. praying   d. sleeping

5. Her accusers were:
   a. Pharisees and scribes
   b. Jesus' disciples
   c. her husband and father-in-law
   d. an angry mob

6. "Now _____ in the law commanded us, that such should be stoned: but what sayest thou?"

7. True or False: The woman's accusers were genuinely attempting to seek an answer from Jesus.

8. Was there any doubt as to the woman's guilt?

9. What did Jesus write in the sand?

10. As Jesus wrote, the woman's accusers:
    a. fell silent
    b. kept asking the question
    c. tried to read what he was writing
    d. wandered around the vicinity collecting stones

11. "He lifted up himself, and said unto them, He that is without sin among you, let him first cast a _____ at her."

12. After Jesus said this, He:
    a. began writing on the ground again
    b. prayed
    c. placed His hand upon her forehead to cast out a demon
    d. wept

13. People in the crowd were convicted by
    what?

14. The first in the crowd to leave was:
    a. the youngest
    b. the eldest
    c. the chief scribe
    d. the woman

15. "When Jesus had lifted up himself, and saw
    none but the woman, he said unto her,
    Woman, where are those thine accusers?
    hath no man condemned thee? She said, No
    man, Lord. And Jesus said unto her, Neither
    do I condemn thee: go, and _____ ____
    _____."

~

I sinned, but because of Jesus, I was set free
from death. Think about how He set you free
from death by dying on the cross in your place.

Can you think of any sin in your life that is
particularly troublesome to you? Ponder what
Jesus said. "Go and sin no more."

Oh, I almost forgot. Here is your

earthenware pot. I hope you will not find it too difficult to cook while you are here.

A priest is upon us.
I shall depart since I don't seem to get along very well with the rabbinical class.

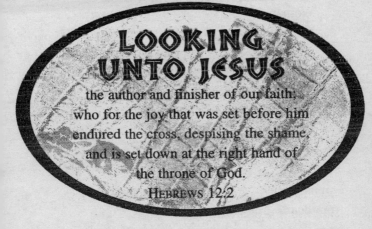

LOOKING UNTO JESUS
the author and finisher of our faith;
who for the joy that was set before him
endured the cross, despising the shame,
and is set down at the right hand of
the throne of God.
HEBREWS 12:2

QUIZ SIXTEEN ANSWERS

I am the adulteress forgiven by the Lord.

1. False. The record of this event appears only in John, chapter 8.
2. c. on the Mount of Olives (John 8:1–3)
3. The temple (John 8:1). This verse says Jesus was teaching in the temple. However, the incident apparently occurred in an outer temple courtyard since Jesus wrote in the sand.
4. c. teaching (John 8:2–3)
5. a. Pharisees and scribes (John 8:3)
6. Moses (John 8:5)
7. False. They were trying to trick Him (John 8:6).
8. No (John 8:4)
9. The Bible doesn't tell us what He wrote (John 8:6).
10. b. kept asking the question (John 8:7).
11. Stone (John 8:7)
12. a. began writing on the ground again (John 8:8)
13. Their conscience (John 8:9)
14. b. the eldest (John 8:9)
15. Sin no more (John 8:11)

QUIZ SEVENTEEN

Good evening. I feel a chill in the air as night approaches. I prophesy that you will need a coat to keep you warm. If you demonstrate how much you remember about me, I will grant you a coat much like the ones my mother fashioned for me when I was a child.

My name is _____.

1. Who was Samuel's mother?

2. Hannah:
   a. prayed to bear a son
   b. made him a coat each year
   c. presented him to Eli after he was weaned
   d. all of the above

3. Why was Samuel chosen to be a judge over Eli's sons?

4. At the time, with whom was Israel at war?

5. The enemies captured:
   a. the ark of God
   b. the gold in the treasury
   c. the slaves of the Israelites
   d. Eli and Samuel

6. During this battle, what prophecy of the Lord came to pass?
   a. Saul was crowned king
   b. Eli's sons died
   c. the temple was destroyed
   d. the Israelites returned to God

7. Was the Israelites' property returned during Samuel's rule?

8. To regain God's favor, Samuel told the Israelites to:
    a. increase their tithes
    b. put away false gods
    c. both of the above
    d. neither of the above

9. True or False: God protected Israel from the Philistines during Samuel's tenure.

10. Whom did Samuel appoint as judges after he grew old?

11. The new judges:
    a. were righteous
    b. took bribes
    c. appointed women in their stead
    d. killed Samuel

12. "And the LORD said unto Samuel, Hearken unto the voice of the people in all that they say unto thee: for they have not rejected thee, but they have rejected ____, that I should not reign over them."

13. True or False: Samuel warned the Israelites what would happen to them under the rule of a king.

14. Who was sent to anoint Saul as king?

15. Who summoned Samuel from the dead?

❧

My prediction was correct. You earned the coat.

As you can see from the events surrounding my life, each person must come to the Lord through his or her own volition. Eli was righteous, but his sons were evil, and so I was anointed a judge in their stead. Likewise I followed the Lord, but I regret that my sons did not.

Do you know someone who was raised in the Christian faith but fell away? How about someone who was not raised as a Christian but still came to know the Lord? Pray today for those who have fallen away. Pray also for those who know the Lord to remain steadfast in their walk with Him.

I see someone approaching
in the distance. I wish you well
on your next test.

God does not have grandchildren.
Each person must come to the Lord
on his or her own.

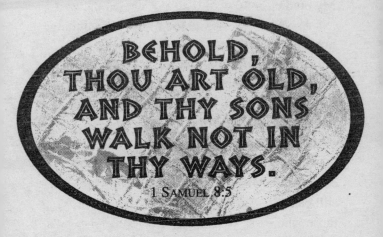

BEHOLD,
THOU ART OLD,
AND THY SONS
WALK NOT IN
THY WAYS.

1 Samuel 8:5

QUIZ SEVENTEEN ANSWERS

My name is Samuel.

1. Hannah (1 Samuel 1:20)
2. d. all of the above (1 Samuel 1:11, 2:19, 1:24–25)
3. Eli's sons were evil (1 Samuel 2:12).
4. The Philistines (1 Samuel 4:1)
5. a. the ark of God (1 Samuel 4:11)
6. b. Eli's sons died (1 Samuel 2:34, 4:11)
7. Yes (1 Samuel 6:3)
8. b. put away false gods (1 Samuel 7:3)
9. True (1 Samuel 7:13)
10. His sons (1 Samuel 8:1)
11. b. took bribes (1 Samuel 8:3)
12. Me (1 Samuel 8:7)
13. True (1 Samuel 8:11–18)
14. Samuel (1 Samuel 9:27–10:1)
15. Saul (1 Samuel 28:15), with help of the witch of En-dor (1 Samuel 28:7).

QUIZ EIGHTEEN

Congratulations! You're well over halfway through the challenges. I trust they didn't prove too much of a sacrifice. I was almost sacrificed myself, but an angel saved my life.

Now let me present you with a few questions. Answer thirteen or more correctly, and a knife will be your prize.

My name is _____.

1. Why was Isaac's birth a miracle?

2. Abraham circumcised Isaac when Isaac was:
   a. eight hours old
   b. seven days old
   c. eight days old
   d. thirteen years old

3. How old was Isaac's father, Abraham, when Isaac was born?

4. What did the Lord ask Abraham to do as a sign of his faith?

5. Abraham was stopped from this act by:
   a. God's angel
   b. Isaac's rebellion
   c. one of Abraham's servants
   d. Sarah

6. True or False: Isaac chose Rebekah as his wife.

7. Can you name the twins Isaac fathered?

8. Why did Isaac tell Abimelech that Rebekah was his sister rather than his wife?

9. True or False: God demonstrated His faithfulness to Isaac by blessing him with fruitful land and many flocks and servants.

10. God renewed His covenant with Isaac because:
    a. his father, Abraham, had been faithful to Him
    b. Isaac had been faithful
    c. Isaac had intervened for his uncle Lot
    d. Isaac had always presented Him with generous burnt offerings

11. True or False: Isaac approved of Esau's marriages to Judith and Bashemath.

12. Who was Isaac's favorite son?

13. Why did Isaac send Jacob away?

14. Isaac's half brother was:
    a. Joseph
    b. Jacob
    c. Ishmael
    d. Lot

15. Isaac lived to the age of:
    a. 100
    b. 150
    c. 180
    d. 300

~

Welcome back. I see you did well on the quiz. I present you with this knife. Put it to good use.

My life illustrates how a family's faithfulness to God is rewarded. My father loved the Lord enough to sacrifice me to Him, even though my parents had waited all their lives for a son.

What is the most challenging commandment for you? How is your life better because of your faithfulness?

Although God asked Abraham to surrender his only son, He stopped Abraham from going through with the sacrifice once He could see Abraham was faithful to Him. However, God goes even further for us.

John 3:16: "For God so loved the world, that he gave his only begotten Son, that whosoever believeth in him should not perish, but have everlasting life." This verse is one to remember every day.

Behold, I see fishermen
casting their nets. I am told
one of them has a test for you.

God rewards those who keep
His commandments.

HONOUR THY
FATHER AND
THY MOTHER.
EXODUS 20:12

QUIZ EIGHTEEN ANSWERS

My name is Isaac.

1. His mother, Sarah, was ninety years old when she received the news she would give birth to a child (Genesis 17:17).
2. c. eight days old (Genesis 21:4)
3. One hundred years old (Genesis 21:5)
4. The Lord asked Abraham to offer Isaac as a burnt sacrifice to Him (Genesis 22:2).
5. a. God's angel (Genesis 22:11–12)
6. False. Rebekah was chosen for him. (Genesis 24)
7. Esau and Jacob (Genesis 25:24–26)
8. Isaac was afraid he would be killed by men who would want the beautiful Rebekah as their own (Genesis 26:7–9).
9. True (Genesis 26:12–14)
10. a. his father, Abraham, had been faithful to Him (Genesis 26:5)
11. False (Genesis 26:34–35)
12. Esau (Genesis 25:28)
13. Rebekah told Isaac that her life would be no good to her if Jacob married a local girl (Genesis 27:46).
14. c. Ishmael (Genesis 25:8–9)
15. c. 180 (Genesis 35:28)

QUIZ NINETEEN

Greetings. I am one of the disciples of Jesus of Nazareth, the Son of God. He told me and my brother that we would be fishers of men.

I was not a perfect disciple, as shown when I denied Jesus. However, after His resurrection, I spread the good news about Him.

If you can successfully complete the quiz about me, I'll give you a fishing pole so you can catch your own fish. I trust since you have made it this far, you are spiritually equipped to fish for the men and women of your generation, proclaiming the gospel everywhere.

My name is _____.

1. Before he became a disciple of Jesus, how did Peter make a living?

2. "And he saith unto them, Follow me, and I will make you _____ of men."

3. What was Peter's alternative name?

4. Jesus healed Peter's mother-in-law of:
   a. leprosy
   b. demon possession
   c. blindness
   d. a fever

5. How did Peter answer Jesus' question, "But whom say you that I am?"

6. "And I say also unto thee, That thou art Peter, and upon this _____ I will build my church; and the gates of hell shall not prevail against it."

7. Why did Jesus say to Peter, "Get thee behind me Satan"?

8. Jesus gave Peter:
   a. the keys to the kingdom of heaven
   b. His robe
   c. the honor of saying Peter was the greatest disciple
   d. the gift of prophecy

9. True or False: Peter witnessed the transfiguration, along with James and John.

10. Upon Jesus' instruction, Peter acquired money for the temple tax from:
    a. a sympathetic priest
    b. the carcass of a lion
    c. the mouth of a fish
    d. the jaw of a donkey

11. True or False: Peter asked Jesus how many times he was required to forgive his brother.

12. Jesus said Peter would deny the Christ how many times before the cock crowed?

13. Was Peter with Jesus at the Garden of Gethsemane?

14. When Jesus was being arrested, Peter cut off the high priest's servant's:
    a. thumb   c. beard
    b. ear   d. arm

15. How many times did Jesus ask Peter if he loved Jesus more than the other disciples loved Him?

~

Oh, there you are. Sorry I fell asleep. As the Lord said to me at the Garden of Gethsemane, "the spirit indeed is willing, but the flesh is weak." The best among us may fall when tempted, or simply from exhaustion. I hope you now see that my repentance and later mission work for the Lord show that erring does not always mean defeat. When one truly loves Him, He will provide.

Read more about me in the book of Acts. I also wrote two epistles that bear my name.

As my denials show, it is tempting to disregard a rule of God that seems inconvenient or inexpedient. How do you face these temptations?

Since you were successful in answering
the questions about my life, here is
your fishing pole. Of course, my brother
and I used nets, but catching fish one
at a time should be sufficient to sustain
you. And should you tire of fish, I
understand next you will have a chance
to earn a slingshot. The game is
quite plentiful here.

The Lord provides!

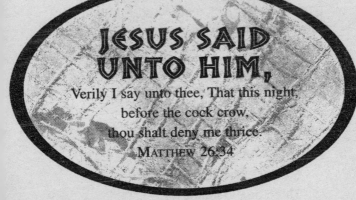

JESUS SAID
UNTO HIM,
Verily I say unto thee, That this night,
before the cock crow,
thou shalt deny me thrice.
MATTHEW 26:34

QUIZ NINETEEN ANSWERS

My name is Peter.

1. He was a fisherman (Matthew 4:18).
2. Fishers (Matthew 4:19)
3. Simon (Matthew 4:18)
4. d. a fever (Mark 1:30–31)
5. "Thou art the Christ" (Mark 8:29).
6. Rock (Matthew 16:18)
7. Because Peter said Jesus need not be tested by the religious leaders of His day, suffer the cross, and then rise on the third day. Jesus protested that Peter was denying the will of God (Matthew 16:21–23).
8. a. the keys to heaven (Matthew 16:19)
9. True (Luke 9:28–29; Matthew 17:1–13; Mark 9:2–10)
10. c. the mouth of a fish (Matthew 17:27)
11. True (Matthew 18:21). Jesus teaches this lesson again in Luke 17:3–4. However, this passage does not indicate that Peter asked the question.
12. Three (John 13:38)
13. Yes (Matthew 26:36–37; Mark 14:32–33)
14. b. ear (Matthew 26:51; Mark 14:47; Luke 22:50–51; John 18:10)
15. Three times (John 21:15–17)

QUIZ TWENTY

Hello. I see you've made it this far. Congratulations. Not that I'm surprised. God allows His servants to overcome impossible odds. Take my battle with Goliath. No one thought I'd come out alive. Little did they know about my faith!

Now that you have fire and oil, I trust you're eager for some meat. If you pass this test about me, your reward will be a slingshot. Happy hunting!

I am _____.

1. David was anointed king after the Lord:
    a. killed Saul for falling away
       from Him
    b. rejected Saul from being king
    c. reinstituted the rule of judges
    d. gave David victory over the Syrians

2. When Saul was troubled by an evil spirit,
   David played the:
    a. harp
    b. sitar
    c. horn
    d. tambourine

3. Name the giant David slew.

4. True or False: David married Saul's eldest
   daughter, Merab.

5. To win Saul's daughter, Saul challenged
   David to:
    a. steal the royal garb of the Philistine
       king
    b. cut off Pharaoh's thumbs
    c. scope out the land of Canaan with
       several other spies
    d. bring him one hundred Philistine
       foreskins

6. True or False: By the time David won Saul's daughter, Saul was already jealous of him.

7. With whom did David make a covenant to protect each other?

8. "And Saul cast a javelin at him to smite him: whereby Jonathan knew that it was determined of his father to slay ____ ____."

9. After Saul's death, David was made king of:
   a. Judah
   b. Gilead
   c. Israel
   d. all of the above

10. True or False: After the death of Saul's sons, David reigned over Israel.

11. When David reproached Michal for criticizing his dancing, David was celebrating:
   a. Passover
   b. Purim
   c. the return of God's ark
   d. Saul's death

12. In remembrance of Jonathan, what did
    David do for Jonathan's son
    Mephibosheth?

13. Mephiboseth was:
    a. blind
    b. lame in both feet
    c. a leper
    d. deaf

14. Who was king after David?

15. To which book of the Bible did David
    heavily contribute?

~

You probably remember reading when you
were a child about my victory over Goliath.
Perhaps you are less familiar with my many
triumphs in later battles as I gained power and
expanded my kingdom. My chances for victory
were not always assured beforehand, but I won
because I was anointed by the Lord.

    Do you remember a time in your life when
you faced impossible odds? What did you do?

Think about how you relied on the Lord for help and guidance.

Behold! On the horizon is a friend who turned into a bitter enemy. Let me leave you now, lest we meet with conflict.

God helps His servants overcome impossible odds.

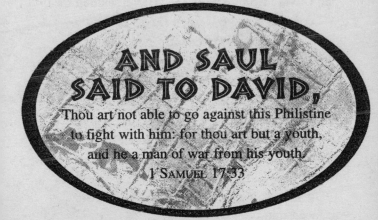

AND SAUL SAID TO DAVID, Thou art not able to go against this Philistine to fight with him: for thou art but a youth, and he a man of war from his youth.

1 SAMUEL 17:33

QUIZ TWENTY ANSWERS

I am David.

1. b. rejected Saul from being king
   (1 Samuel 16:1)
2. a. harp (1 Samuel 16:23)
3. Goliath (1 Samuel 17:23)
4. False. He eventually married a younger
   daughter, Michal, because they loved each
   other (1 Samuel 18:20).
5. d. bring him one hundred Philistine fore-
   skins (1 Samuel 18:25)
6. True (1 Samuel 18:25)
7. Saul's son Jonathan (1 Samuel 20:1–23)
8. David (1 Samuel 20:33). After Jonathan discovered this, he warned David as they
   agreed in their covenant.
9. a. Judah (2 Samuel 2:7)
10. True (2 Samuel 5:1–5)
11. c. the return of God's ark (2 Samuel 6:16)
12. David provided for his needs and allowed
    him to dine at his table (2 Samuel 9:6–13).
13. b. lame in both feet (2 Samuel 6:13)
14. Solomon (1 Kings 1:30)
15. David is credited with writing most of
    the Psalms.

QUIZ TWENTY-ONE

Shalom. I see you've visited with David. And what did my protégé give you? A slingshot? A crude instrument of war indeed. And to think, the women sang that he killed more men in battle than did I!

If you can pass this test about me, a rich and powerful king, one chosen by God, I offer you a bow and a quiver full of arrows. These weapons will prove far superior to David's mere slingshot, I assure you. I wish you Godspeed.

My name is _____.

1. Saul's story begins in what book of the Bible?

2. Saul is described as:
   a. goodly and tall
   b. short but comely
   c. ruddy and robust
   d. handsome and a scholar

3. When the Lord told Samuel to anoint Saul, his mission was to:
   a. deliver his people out of the hand of the Philistines
   b. expand the Lord's territory
   c. convert the local pagans to Judaism
   d. deliver the Israelites from the Egyptians

4. From which tribe was Saul?

5. True or False: Saul was surprised to be selected because his tribe was the smallest.

6. Why did the Lord regret choosing Saul?

7. Saul enjoyed David because:
    a. David's music would provide good entertainment for his parties
    b. David's music would soothe Saul when an evil spirit tormented him
    c. he wanted to hear David's psalms
    d. they were both warriors

8. Saul became jealous of David because:
    a. he was more handsome
    b. he was taller
    c. his harem was larger
    d. the women sang that he had killed more people in battle

9. To the man who killed Goliath, Saul promised to:
    a. enrich him with great riches
    b. give him his daughter
    c. make his father's house free in Israel
    d. all of the above

10. True or False: Once David killed Goliath, Saul happily gave him his daughter Michal's hand in marriage.

11. When David spared Saul's life, he:
    a. cut off the skirt of his robe
    b. braided his hair as he slept
    c. snipped off the tip of his beard
    d. tied his hands together

12. Why did David spare Saul's life twice?

13. After Saul got no answer from the Lord or the prophets about the war with the Philistines, he consulted:
    a. Samuel
    c. Joab
    b. David
    d. Goliath

14. Why was consulting this person so unusual at the time?

15. After Saul died, who became king of Judah?

❧

Although I was anointed king by the Lord, my fall from the faith was my undoing. After I abandoned the Lord, I let my envy of David guide my life.

All of us fall prey to envy from time to time. Saul's life shows the negative outcomes of envy.

His animosity toward David caused Saul to make decisions calculated to hurt and defeat David. Could Saul have taken his envy and used it to encourage him to better himself? Think about this the next time you feel envious.

Despite the fact that Saul was David's enemy, David did not treat Saul's murderer kindly (2 Samuel 1:13–16).

Hark! I behold a disciple of Christ.
I shall leave you to your next test.

Do not envy.

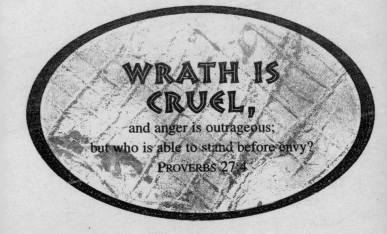

WRATH IS CRUEL, and anger is outrageous; but who is able to stand before envy?
PROVERBS 27:4

QUIZ TWENTY-ONE ANSWERS

My name is Saul.

1. 1 Samuel
2. a. goodly and tall (1 Samuel 9:2)
3. a. deliver his people out of the hands of the Philistines (1 Samuel 9:16)
4. Benjamin (1 Samuel 9:16)
5. True (1 Samuel 9:21)
6. Because Saul rejected the word of the Lord (1 Samuel 15:26)
7. b. David's music would soothe Saul (1 Samuel 16:23)
8. d. the women sang that he had killed more people in battle (1 Samuel 29:5)
9. d. all of the above (1 Samuel 17:25)
10. False (1 Samuel 18:25)
11. a. cut his robe (1 Samuel 24:11)
12. Because Saul was anointed by the Lord (1 Samuel 24:6, 26:9)
13. a. Samuel (1 Samuel 28:15)
14. Samuel was dead. Saul went to a woman with a familiar spirit. (Read about the story in 1 Samuel 28:7–25.)
15. David (2 Samuel 2:4)

QUIZ TWENTY-TWO

Good evening. Surely you're ready to eat again by now. If you can show you remember what the Bible says about me, the beloved disciple, I'll give you a small rowboat so you can fish for your dinner.

I was a fisherman by trade. But when I began following Jesus Christ, I became a fisher of men.

I am _____.

1. "In the beginning was the _____, and the
   _____ was with God, and the _____
   was God."

2. The authorship of the book of John is
   traditionally attributed to whom?

3. The beloved disciple in John 13:23 is:
   a. John
   b. Peter
   c. James
   d. Andrew

4. The disciple who was John's brother was
   named _____.

5. True or False: John was the first disciple
   called by Jesus.

6. What was John's profession?

7. When John was called, he was with his:
   a. wife
   b. father
   c. mother
   d. uncle

8. True or False: When John was called, he was hesitant because Jesus told him He had no place to lay His head.

9. Peter, James, and John saw Jesus raise whose daughter from the dead?

10. When Jesus experienced the transfiguration witnessed by John, Peter, and James, those who appeared unto Jesus were:
    a. Elijah and Elisha
    b. John the Baptist and Moses
    c. Abraham and Moses
    d. Moses and Elijah

11. Who asked Jesus to let the sons of Zebedee sit at each side of Jesus in His kingdom?

12. True or False: John wrote down everything that Jesus did.

13. Which of John's letters includes the beautiful instruction, "Beloved, let us love one another"?

14. Why were John and Peter imprisoned after Jesus' resurrection?

15. Where was John when he received the Revelation of Jesus?

If you answered at least thirteen questions, congratulations! The rowboat is yours. I spent many a day on my boat before Jesus called me to follow Him. Little did I know I would change from an ordinary fisherman to the most beloved disciple of Christ.

John didn't hesitate to follow Jesus, but his example isn't always easy to follow. Has God ever asked you to do something, and you were reluctant to follow His will? If you followed His plan, what blessings did you receive?

Take your boat and journey down the river. Not only will you find fish, but a woman waiting, with another test.

Jesus does not always seek
the most important or worldly,
but those who will follow Him willingly.

AND HE SAITH

unto them, Follow me,
and I will make you fishers of men.
And they straightway left their nets,
and followed him.
MATTHEW 4:19–20

QUIZ TWENTY-TWO ANSWERS

I am John the Apostle.

1. Word, Word, Word (John 1:1)
2. John, the son of Zebedee, also known as John the Apostle
3. a. John (John 13:23; also see John 21:7)
4. James (Matthew 4:21)
5. False. Peter and Andrew, two fishermen brothers, were called first (Matthew 4:18; Mark 1:16–20).
6. He was a fisherman (Matthew 4:21).
7. b. father (Matthew 4:21–22; Mark 1:20)
8. False. John immediately accepted the call (Matthew 4:21–22).
9. Jairus, the ruler of the synagogue (Luke 8:41–55)
10. d. Moses and Elijah (Elias) (Mark 9:4)
11. Their mother (Matthew 20:20–21)
12. False. "There are also many other things which Jesus did" (John 21:25).
13. 1 John (4:7)
14. For preaching the gospel (Acts 4:1–4)
15. Exiled on the island of Patmos (Revelation 1:9)

QUIZ TWENTY-THREE

Good morning. Certainly you recognize me. I gave King David a son who went on to be part of the line of Jesus Christ.

I lived much of my life amidst great wealth. I see that your clothing has become worn and dirty over the course of your stay here. I have fine clothing to give you, should you prove your wit as to my story. Let us see how much you know.

My name is _____ _____.

1. Bathsheba's story begins in:
   a. 1 Samuel   c. 1 Kings
   b. 2 Samuel   d. 2 Kings

2. Where was David when he first spied Bathsheba?

3. What was Bathsheba doing at the time?

4. True or False: After David sent a messenger to reveal her identity to him, David lay with her and then she returned to her house.

5. After Bathsheba conceived, David contacted what army leader to summon Bathsheba's husband from the battlefront?
   a. Joab   c. Saul
   b. Uriah   d. Naaman

6. By bringing Bathsheba's husband home, David hoped:
   a. to bribe him to remain quiet about David's indiscretion with his wife
   b. that he would sleep with Bathsheba so he would think the baby was his
   c. kill him
   d. imprison him on false charges so David could marry Bathsheba

7. After her husband's death, Bathsheba:
   a. mourned her husband
   b. went to live with David
   c. bore a son
   d. all of the above

8. True or False. Bathsheba's baby died.

9. "And David comforted Bathsheba his wife, and went in unto her, and lay with her: and she bare a son, and he called his name _____: and the LORD loved him."

10. After David had become old and Adonijah tried to seize the throne, Nathan asked _____ to talk to the king on Solomon's behalf.

11. True or False: Nathan told Solomon's mother that if Adonijah was allowed to rule, both her life and Solomon's would be at stake.

12. Nathan had played a role in their lives earlier when he:
   a. sent Bathsheba's husband on a suicide mission

    b. used a story to reveal to David the Lord's displeasure with his sin

    c. advised David how to win the war against the Ammonites

    d. saved the country from famine by interpreting a dream

13. Who spoke to David about the person who would inherit the throne?

    a. Solomon and Bathsheba

    b. Solomon and Nathan

    c. Nathan and Bathsheba

    d. Bathsheba and Adonijah

14. True or False: David promised that Solomon would reign after him.

15. What Psalm recounts the confession of David after his sin with Bathsheba?

If you answered at least thirteen questions correctly, you earned a new set of clothing. Congratulations. Now you can see how God forgives sin, no matter how great. Not only did He show forgiveness to me with the birth of Solomon, but also to David.

Those who believe in God experience His forgiveness in all things. But can you recall a time in your life when you especially felt His love and forgiveness?

Meditate upon that for a few moments before you proceed to the next test.

Forgiveness of sin can be found in the Lord.

THE NEXT DAY

John seeth Jesus coming unto him, and saith, Behold the Lamb of God, which taketh away the sin of the world.

JOHN 1:29

QUIZ TWENTY-THREE ANSWERS

My name is Bathsheba.

1. b. 2 Samuel
2. He was on the roof of the king's house
   (2 Samuel 11:2).
3. She was taking a bath (2 Samuel 11:2).
4. True (2 Samuel 11:4)
5. a. Joab (2 Samuel 11:6)
6. b. that he would sleep with Bathsheba so
   he would think the baby was his
   (2 Samuel 11:10)
7. d. all of the above (2 Samuel 11:26–27)
8. True (2 Samuel 12:19)
9. Solomon (2 Samuel 12:24)
10. Bathsheba (1 Kings 1:11–12)
11. True (1 Kings 1:12)
12. b. used a story to reveal to David the
    Lord's displeasure with his sin
    (2 Samuel 12:1–14)
13. c. Nathan and Bathsheba (1 Kings 1:22)
14. True (1 Kings 1:30)
15. Psalm 51

QUIZ TWENTY-FOUR

Grace to you. My, but you've come this far, and you have no beast to take you over the land? How tired you must be!

Answer ten of the following questions about me correctly, and I'll present you with a fine donkey. Trust me, your journey will be much easier with his help. Oh, by the way, could you deliver this epistle to Timothy?

My name is _____.

1. We first meet Paul in:
   - a. Luke
   - b. John
   - c. Romans
   - d. The Acts of the Apostles

2. True or False: Paul was present at Stephen's stoning.

3. When Paul was traveling to Damascus, he was converted to Christianity even though he was on his way there to:
   - a. build a temple
   - b. teach the Torah
   - c. see the trial of Stephen
   - d. bring Christians back to Jerusalem as prisoners

4. "But the Lord said unto him, Go thy way: for he is a chosen vessel unto me, to bear my name before the _____, and kings, and the children of Israel."

5. True or False: When Paul first began preaching the gospel, the Jewish leaders did not oppose him.

6. Was Paul a member of the Sadducees or the Pharisees?

7. The Pharisees believed in:
    a. life after death and the supernatural
    b. life after death, but not angels
    c. neither life after death nor the supernatural
    d. angels, but not in life after death

8. True or False: Despite being passed from one official to another, Paul's case never came to trial.

9. As a result of the events surrounding Paul's case as recorded in Acts:
    a. the Jews stopped harassing him
    b. as a people, the Jews rejected Christ as Lord and Messiah
    c. the Christian church began to become a religion of Gentiles
    d. all of the above

10. True or False: Paul always described himself in his letters as head of the church.

11. Which of Paul's letters includes the famous charge, "Study to show thyself approved unto God"?

12. True or False: Without doubt, Paul wrote the epistle to the Hebrews.

13. "Yea, and all that will live godly in Christ Jesus shall suffer _____."

14. *"Stand therefore, having your loins girt about with truth, and having on the breastplate of righteousness; and your feet shod with the preparation of the gospel of peace; above all, taking the shield of faith, wherewith ye shall be able to quench all the fiery darts of the wicked. And take the helmet of salvation, and the sword of the Spirit, which is the word of God"* (Ephesians 6:14–17). What is Paul describing?

15. What is the one quality Paul told the Corinthians a Christian must have?

So you knew enough about me to earn the donkey, eh? Take good care of her.

As you now know, I wasn't always an apostle of Jesus. But He turned my hardened heart toward His face. Though I was persecuted for talking about Him, my reward is eternal life.

Is there someone in your life who doesn't know Christ? Have you given up on ever reaching that person for the Lord? Pray about it and watch what God does.

Behold, I see a woman in the distance. I wonder what she wants to know?

Even the most hard-hearted may find the Lord.

BUT THE LORD

said unto him, Go thy way: for [Saul] is a chosen vessel unto me, to bear my name before the Gentiles, and kings, and the children of Israel.

ACTS 9:15

QUIZ TWENTY-FOUR ANSWERS

My name is Paul.

1. d. The Acts of the Apostles. (His story starts in Acts 7:58.)
2. True (Acts 7:58–8:1)
3. d. bring Christians back to Jerusalem as prisoners (Acts 9:1–2)
4. Gentiles (Acts 9:15)
5. False (Acts 9:20–23)
6. The Pharisees (Acts 23:6)
7. a. in life after death and the supernatural (Acts 23:6–9)
8. True. The fact that Luke does not record the trial and exonerate Paul indicates that a trial never took place.
9. d. all of the above (Acts 28:27–31)
10. False. He referred to himself as a servant of Christ (Romans 1:1; Titus 1:1).
11. 2 Timothy (2:15)
12. False. Although this epistle deals with matters of the early church, the author does not tell his readers that he is an apostle.
13. Persecution (2 Timothy 3:12)
14. The whole armor of God (Ephesians 6:13)
15. Charity; or, in recent translations, love (1 Corinthians 13:1–13)

QUIZ TWENTY-FIVE

Peace to you. I've been told you have most of the material goods you need for survival. I am here to give you a greater gift—that of courage. If you don't know my story already, you'll soon see how my courage—my decision to reach out and touch Someone—was rewarded by the Lord Himself.

I am _____.

1. True or False: All four Gospels relate the story of the woman who touched the garment of Jesus.

2. What was Jesus doing when His garment was touched?

3. The woman suffered from:
    a. deafness
    b. demon possession
    c. leprosy
    d. a bleeding condition

4. How long had she been suffering?

5. The woman was so desperate to rid herself of the disorder that she:
    a. consulted the dead
    b. saw a witch doctor
    c. wore garlic around her neck
    d. spent all her money on doctors

6. "For she said within herself, If I may but _____ his garment, I shall be whole."

7. She touched Jesus':
    a. girdle   c. sandal
    b. sash   d. hem

8. According to Mark, when she made contact with His garment, what did Jesus say?

9. In response, Luke writes that the disciples said:
   a. "Move aside, away from the Master."
   b. "Master, the multitude throng thee and press thee."
   c. "Master, how dareth anyone touch thee!"
   d. "Get thee behind me, Satan."

10. Jesus knew the touch was no accident. Why?

11. Seeing she was discovered, the woman:
   a. trembled
   b. bowed and worshiped Him
   c. confessed
   d. all of the above

12. Jesus called her:
   a. daughter
   b. woman
   c. Mary
   d. sister

13. True or False: Her faith had made her well.

14. True or False: According to Luke, she was healed immediately.

15. Jesus told her, "Go in _____."

I heard about Jesus and touched His garment to become well. When I was found out, I summoned all my courage to confess. I hope my story has inspired you to be courageous.

Was there ever a time your faith walk took you to a place where you were afraid? What did you do? How did the Lord help?

Behold, a man approacheth.
I bid you farewell.

Surviving requires courage.

BE STRONG
and of a good courage,
fear not, nor be afraid of them;
for the LORD thy God, he it is that doth go with
thee; he will not fail thee, nor forsake thee.

DEUTERONOMY 31:6

QUIZ TWENTY-FIVE ANSWERS

I am the bleeding woman; or, the woman who touched Jesus' garment.

1. False Her story is recorded in Matthew, chapter 9; Mark, chapter 5; and Luke, chapter 8. John doesn't mention this healing.
2. He was on his way to heal the synagogue leader's daughter (Matthew 9:18–20).
3. d. a bleeding condition (Matthew 9:20; Mark 5:25; Luke 8:43)
4. Twelve years (Luke 8:43; Mark 5:25)
5. d. spent all her money on doctors (Mark 5:26; Luke 8:43)
6. Touch (Matthew 9:21)
7. d. hem (Matthew 9:20; Luke 8:44)
8. "Who touched my clothes?" (Mark 5:30)
9. b. "Master, the multitude throng thee and press thee" (Luke 8:45).
10. He felt virtue leave Him (Mark 5:30).
11. d. all of the above (Mark 5:33; Luke 8:47)
12. a. daughter (Matthew 9:22; Mark 5:34)
13. True (Matthew 9:22; Mark 5:34; Luke 8:48)
14. True (Luke 8:47)
15. Peace (Mark 5:34; Luke 8:48)

QUIZ TWENTY-SIX

Good evening. I am told you already have a coat from Samuel to shield you from the evening chill as you move about. But you shall need to stay warm as you sleep. Believe me, I didn't sleep much when I was thrown into the lions' den. But God kept me safe.

Answer the following questions about me, and a covering made of lion skin will be your reward.

My name is _____.

1. True or False: Nebuchadnezzar was king of Babylon.

2. Daniel became a part of the king's court because he was:
    a. an Israelite
    b. of royal blood
    c. unblemished
    d. all of the above

3. True or False: Daniel did not eat the king's food, although his friends did.

4. What special gift did God give Daniel?

5. How did Daniel gain King Nebuchadnezzar's favor?

6. After Daniel gained the king's favor, the king:
    a. worshiped Daniel
    b. praised Daniel's God
    c. gave Daniel gifts
    d. all of the above

7. True or False: Daniel became ruler of Babylon.

8. Nebuchadnezzar required everyone to worship an image of:
   a. stone
   b. gold
   c. silver
   d. bronze

9. "But if not, be it known unto thee, O king, that we will not serve thy gods, nor _____ the golden image which thou hast set up."

10. True or False: Daniel was among the men the Lord saved from the fiery furnace.

11. A later king, Darius, signed a decree that no one was to pray to any God but him for how many days?

12. As a result of this decree, did Daniel's prayer habits change?

13. After Darius saw how the decree affected Daniel, he:
    a. retracted it
    b. made it effective for the rest of his reign
    c. was unable to change it according to the law of the Medes and Persians
    d. tore up the document and threw it in the fire

14. "Then the king commanded, and they brought Daniel, and cast him into the den of lions. Now the king spake and said unto Daniel, Thy God whom thou servest continually, he will _____ thee."

15. After Daniel was delivered from the lions' den, the king:
    a. proclaimed God
    b. killed the men who tricked him into signing the decree, and their families
    c. both of the above
    d. none of the above

Congratulations on the demonstration of your knowledge. As a reward, I present you with this lion skin.

As you can see, obeying God can mean risking your life. But He protects those who do His will.

Can you recall a time when you were afraid? What did you do? How did God help you?

I leave you now. Someone else is
approaching. Be strong. . .
your journey is nearing completion.

Those who love the Lord have nothing to fear.

AND I SAY
unto you my friends,
Be not afraid of them that kill the body,
and after that have no more that they can do.
LUKE 12:4

QUIZ TWENTY-SIX ANSWERS

My name is Daniel.

1. True (Daniel 1:1)
2. d. all of the above (Daniel 1:3–4)
3. False. Neither Daniel nor his friends ate the king's food (Daniel 1:11–14).
4. The ability to understand visions and dreams (Daniel 1:17)
5. He interpreted the king's dream when others could not. Read about it in Daniel 2:12–46.
6. d. all of the above (Daniel 2:46–47)
7. True (Daniel 2:48)
8. b. gold (Daniel 3:1–7)
9. Worship (Daniel 3:18)
10. False (Daniel 3:26)
11. Thirty (Daniel 6:7–9)
12. No (Daniel 6:10)
13. c. was unable to change it according to the law of the Medes and Persians (Daniel 6:15)
14. Deliver (Daniel 6:16)
15. c. both of the above (Daniel 6:24–26)

QUIZ TWENTY-SEVEN

Peace and grace be upon you! You may not remember me, because my story lies deep in the book of Acts. I know you have a new blanket, but sleeping on the bare ground will offer limited comfort. If you can answer the following questions, your reward will be a bed. I can tell you from personal experience, sleeping on a bed is much better than sleeping in a window! You'll see what I mean.

My name is _____.

1. Where can you find the passage on Eutychus?

2. The setting is:
   a. Troy
   b. Troas
   c. Athens
   d. Philippi

3. On what day of the week did the incident occur?

4. How long did Paul's group stay in the city?

5. The Bible says the disciples had gathered to do what?

6. Paul preached until:
   a. midnight
   b. the cows came home
   c. he had raised sixty gold talents to fund his mission trip
   d. Communion was served

7. True or False: Paul was supposed to depart the city the following day.

8. The disciples were gathered:
    a. at the river
    b. around the altar
    c. in a classroom
    d. in the upper chamber

9. True or False: Eutychus was an old woman.

10. Eutychus:
    a. fell asleep in a window
    b. jumped out of a window to prove
        that God would save him
    c. was accidently pushed out of the
        window
    d. fell out of his chair

11. True or False: When Eutychus fell from
    the third loft, he was seriously injured but
    not dead.

12. True or False: We know the subject of
    Paul's sermon was the fruit of the spirit.

13. "And Paul went down, and fell on him, and
    embracing him said, Trouble not your-
    selves; for his _____ is in him."

14. After Eutychus fell and Paul reassured the crowd, how much longer did Paul preach?

15. "And they brought the young man alive, and were not a little _____."

❧

You're back! Good. You earned this bed.

Paul saved me from an untimely physical death. But the Lord Jesus has a much greater gift—that of eternal life. Tell everyone you know about Him! But you might want to make your sermon short so no one in your audience falls asleep.

Hark! A godly woman is here
to challenge you with her test.
I wish you well.

Those who love the Lord shall have eternal life.

HE THAT BELIEVETH and is baptized shall be saved; but he that believeth not shall be damned. MARK 16:16

QUIZ TWENTY-SEVEN ANSWERS

My name is Eutychus.

1. Acts 20:6–12
2. b. Troas (Acts 20:6)
3. The first day of the week (Acts 20:7)
4. Seven days (Acts 20:6)
5. To break bread (Acts 20:7)
6. a. midnight (Acts 20:7)
7. True (Acts 20:7)
8. d. in the upper chamber (Acts 20:8)
9. False. Eutychus was a young man (Acts 20:9).
10. a. fell asleep in a window (Acts 20:9)
11. False (Acts 20:9)
12. False. The Bible doesn't say what Paul preached that night.
13. Life (Acts 20:10)
14. Until daybreak (Acts 20:11)
15. Comforted (Acts 20:12)

QUIZ TWENTY-EIGHT

Hello. How good to see you. I have just returned from the threshing floor. Would you like a loaf of bread made from the grains of rye and barley? I gleaned these grains from the fields of Boaz—and I shall give you the gift of bread if you can show you know my story.

My name is _____.

1. The events in the book of Ruth take place when what group of people ruled Israel?
   a. judges
   b. priests
   c. kings
   d. pharaohs

2. How many people of Naomi's family went to Moab?

3. From what city was Naomi's family?

4. True or False: Naomi's sons were already married when her husband died.

5. What were the names of Naomi's sons?

6. Naomi told her daughters-in-law to stay in Moab after her sons died because:
   a. there was still famine in Israel
   b. the road to Israel was unsafe for beautiful young women to travel
   c. she couldn't bear more sons for them to marry
   d. the Israelites wouldn't accept them

7. After Naomi returned to her home, she told people to call her:
   a. Mara, meaning bitter
   b. Rachel, meaning ewe
   c. Salome, meaning peace
   d. Edna, meaning reborn

8. What grain was being harvested when Naomi and Ruth returned to Bethlehem?

9. True or False: At first, Boaz was angry at Ruth for gleaning because he was worried that his men would pester the beautiful young woman.

10. True or False: Naomi told Ruth to provide a banquet for Boaz.

11. When Naomi gave her instructions on how to endear herself to Boaz, Ruth:
    a. protested that Boaz was too old for her
    b. said he was not her nearest kinsman
    c. said she would do as Naomi instructed
    d. had to be convinced since she had attracted the attention of many men

12. True or False: Boaz immediately proposed marriage to Ruth.

13. When the nearest kinsman gave up his right to the family property, he:
    a. called Boaz a thief
    b. vowed revenge
    c. took off his shoe
    d. all of the above

14. The townswomen said Ruth was more valuable to Naomi than:
    a. seven sons
    b. half the kingdom
    c. seven sons and seven daughters
    d. thirty gold talents

15. After she and Boaz married, Ruth gave birth to a son, Obed. Why is this significant?

~

Did you answer at least thirteen questions correctly? If so, you must know a thing or two about faithfulness. When I left my native country to be with my mother-in-law, the desire to be loyal to her was my motivation. I never dreamed that romance would be my prize.

Have you ever been loyal to someone beyond expectations? Think about how you were rewarded. Perhaps there is someone in your life today who needs your loyalty.

Behold! I see one of the
fathers of the faith. I must depart,
so that he may pose inquiries of his own.

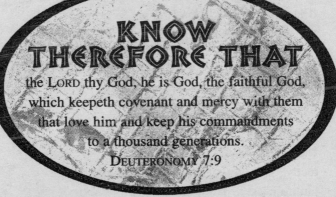

KNOW THEREFORE THAT the LORD thy God, he is God, the faithful God, which keepeth covenant and mercy with them that love him and keep his commandments to a thousand generations.

DEUTERONOMY 7:9

QUIZ TWENTY-EIGHT ANSWERS

My name is Ruth.

1. a. judges (Ruth 1:1)
2. Four people went to Moab: Naomi, her husband, and her two sons, who were unmarried at the time (Ruth 1:1–2).
3. Her family was from Bethlehem-judah (Ruth 1:1).
4. False (Ruth 1:3–4)
5. Their names were Mahlon and Chilion (Ruth 1:2).
6. c. she couldn't bear more sons for them to marry (Ruth 1:11)
7. a. Mara, meaning bitter (Ruth 1:20)
8. Barley was being harvested (Ruth 1:22).
9. False (Ruth 2:7–9)
10. False (Ruth 3:1–3)
11. c. said she would do as Naomi instructed (Ruth 3:5)
12. False (Ruth 3:9–13)
13. c. took off his shoe (Ruth 4:7). This action signaled that the contract was sealed.
14. a. seven sons (Ruth 4:14–15)
15. Obed was the father of Jesse, who was the father of David. Ruth, a Moabitess, was part of the lineage of Jesus Christ (see Matthew 1:5–16).

QUIZ TWENTY-NINE

Shalom. I have heard about you and your expertise regarding the Holy Scriptures. Perhaps the others you have met granted you survival tools. It is my belief that you deserve a few luxuries. How about butter and milk, food fit for an angel?

Speaking of heavenly beings, I was visited by angels who bore incredible news for my wife and me. We learned it's true that "you're never too old to try something new." Find out more by answering a few questions.

I am _____.

1. What was Abraham's name before the LORD changed it?

2. When the LORD told Abram to move from his native land, He promised to:
    a. bless him
    b. make his name great
    c. make him a great nation
    d. all of the above

3. Abram told Sarai (Sarah) to tell the Egyptians that she was his:
    a. wife   c. concubine
    b. sister   d. aunt

4. True or False: Because of Sarai, Pharaoh treated Abraham well, bestowing upon him many gifts that made him a wealthy man.

5. Why did Abram and Lot need to separate?

6. "After these things the word of the _____ came unto Abram in a vision, saying, Fear not, Abram: I am thy shield, and thy exceeding great reward."

7. True or False: Even with God's promise that he would have an heir, Abram worried.

8. "This is my covenant, which ye shall keep, between me and you and thy seed after thee; Every man child among you shall be _____."

9. When Abraham interceded for the wicked city of Sodom, he argued that God shouldn't:
   a. destroy the righteous along with the wicked
   b. destroy the temple in Sodom
   c. send a flood because of His promise to Noah
   d. annihilate the little children

10. True or False: Abraham told Abimelech that Sarah was his sister.

11. What was the name of the son Sarah bore to Abraham when he was old?

12. True or False: Abraham was willing to burn Isaac as a sacrifice to the Lord.

13. Can you name the wife Abraham took after Sarah died?

14. After his death, Abraham's wealth went to:
    a. Isaac
    b. Isaac and Ishmael
    c. all of his sons
    d. his wives

15. "And it came to pass after the death of Abraham, that God blessed his son _____."

~

I see you have returned. Congratulations for responding correctly to at least thirteen questions. You have earned your butter and milk. Enjoy!

As you learned from my life, God sometimes promises things that seem unattainable. Yet when He gives His word, great things happen!

Have you ever been in a situation that seemed hopeless? What happened when you took it to the Lord?

Behold!
In the distance is someone you know.

God lives up to His promises,
even when they seem impossible.

WITH GOD
ALL THINGS
ARE POSSIBLE.
MATTHEW 19:26

QUIZ TWENTY-NINE ANSWERS

I am Abraham.

1. Abram (Genesis 17:5)
2. d. all of the above (Genesis 12:2)
3. b. sister (Genesis 12:13)
4. True (Genesis 12:16)
5. Each possessed so much livestock that the land couldn't support them both (Genesis 13:5–6).
6. LORD (Genesis 15:1)
7. True (Genesis 15:2–3)
8. Circumcised (Genesis 17:10)
9. a. destroy the righteous along with the wicked (Genesis 18:23)
10. True (Genesis 20:2)
11. Isaac (Genesis 21:3)
12. True (Genesis 22:1–12)
13. Keturah (Genesis 25:1)
14. a. Isaac (Genesis 25:5)
15. Isaac (Genesis 25:11)

QUIZ THIRTY

I am the way, the truth, and the life:
no man cometh unto the Father,
but by me.

JOHN 14:6

I am _____ _____.

1. Jesus was born in the town of
   _____.

2. Who gives the most detailed account of the
   events surrounding Jesus' birth?

3. Which Gospel writers record Jesus'
   genealogy?

4. True or False: Jesus taught the Golden Rule.

5. On the Sabbath, Jesus healed a man
   stricken with:
      a. a withered hand
      b. blindness
      c. deafness
      d. paralysis

6. After the healing, who plotted to destroy
   Jesus?

7. What does Jesus want us to know about
   the Sabbath?

8. Jesus taught in stories. What are they called?

9. Why did Jesus use these stories?

10. True or False: Although Jesus was rejected in many cities, He was warmly received in His hometown of Nazareth.

11. Jesus healed the Canaanite woman's daughter because:
    a. her faith was great
    b. He wanted to extend His ministry to the Gentiles
    c. He wanted to show love for enemies
    d. she washed His feet with perfume

12. "God is a _____: and they that worship him must worship him in spirit and in truth."

13. "And Jesus said unto them, I am the _____ of life: he that cometh to me shall never hunger; and he that believeth on me shall never thirst."

14. Which disciple doubted Jesus was risen?

15. Jesus is Alpha and _____.

~

Jesus offers us the ultimate in survival— eternal life!

FOR GOD SO LOVED THE WORLD, THAT HE GAVE HIS ONLY BEGOTTEN SON, THAT WHOSOEVER BELIEVETH IN HIM SHOULD NOT PERISH, BUT HAVE EVERLASTING LIFE.

JOHN 3:16

QUIZ THIRTY ANSWERS

I am the Lord Jesus.

1. Bethlehem (Matthew 2:1; Luke 2:4–7)
2. Luke—read chapters 1–2.
3. Matthew (1:1–17) and Luke (3:23–38)
4. True (Matthew 7:12; Luke 6:31)
5. a. a withered hand (Matthew 12:9–13; Mark 3:1–5; Luke 6:6–10)
6. A group of Pharisees (Matthew 12:14; Mark 3:5; Luke 6:7, 11)
7. "For the Son of man is Lord even of the sabbath day." He owns it (Matthew 12:8; Mark 2:28; Luke 6:5). "Wherefore it is lawful to do well on the sabbath days" (Matthew 12:12).
8. Parables (Matthew 13:3, 13:53, 21:45, 22:1; Mark 3:23, 4:2, 4:33, 12:1)
9. "And the disciples came, and said unto him, Why speakest thou unto them in parables? He answered and said unto them, Because it is given unto you to know the mysteries of the kingdom of heaven, but to them it is not given. For whosoever hath, to him shall be given, and he shall have more abundance: but whosoever hath not, from him shall be taken away even that he hath. Therefore

speak I to them in parables: because they seeing see not; and hearing they hear not, neither do they understand. And in them is fulfilled the prophecy of Esaias, which saith, By hearing ye shall hear, and shall not understand; and seeing ye shall see, and shall not perceive" (Matthew 13:10–14).

    Also see Matthew 13:34–35; Mark 4:11–12; Luke 8:10.

10. False. "And they were offended in him. But Jesus said unto them, A prophet is not without honour, save in his own country, and in his own house" (Matthew 13:57). See also Mark 6:4; John 4:44.

11. a. her faith was great (Matthew 15:21–28; Mark 7:27–30)

12. Spirit (John 4:24)

13. Bread (John 6:35)

14. Thomas (John 20:24–25)

15. Omega (Revelation 1:8, 11; 21:6; 22:13)

CONCLUSION

Success! You have completed *Bible Survival!* You've successfully navigated our challenging course with the help of your survival manual—the Bible—and the encouragement of those who've traveled the path before you. Good job!

You realize, of course, that *Bible Survival* is only a game—but a game with an important point. The fact is, you *will* face trials, temptations, and other traumas in life, just like the characters you've met in these pages. And the Bible is truly your guide not just for surviving, but for surmounting, those trials.

We hope you've enjoyed your time with *Bible Survival.* But even more, we hope we've convinced you of the Bible's importance to your everyday life.

Read it, study it, use it—and share it!

OTHER BIBLE TRIVIA BOOKS
By Tamela Hancock Murray

Great Bible Trivia for Kids
Fun Bible Trivia 2
Fun Bible Trivia 1

Tamela Hancock Murray
NOVELLAS
INCLUDED IN:

City Dreams
Rescue

Available wherever books are sold.
Or order from:

Barbour Publishing, Inc.
P.O. Box 719
Uhrichsville, OH 44683
http://www.barbourbooks.com

If you order by mail add $2.00 to your order for shipping.
Prices subject to change without notice.

FULL-LENGTH ROMANCE NOVELS
By Tamela Hancock Murray

Destinations
The Elusive Mr. Perfect
Picture of Love

With **Heartsong Presents,**
Our Stories are Rated G!
Call 1-800-847-8270
to receive four great full-length
Christian romances, two historical and two contemporary, every month for only $9.97, including postage. You can order Tamela's books separately.

**Tamela
Hancock Murray**
feels privileged to write
for the Christian market.
Her mission is to provide
other Christians with edifying, entertaining works.
This author is grateful to Christian publishers for the opportunity to share unabashedly the saving grace of Jesus Christ. Tamela is represented by Hartline Literary Agency, www.hartlinemarketing.com

LIKE BIBLE TRIVIA?

Then check out these great books from Barbour Publishing!

The Bible Detective by Carol Smith
Solve mysteries posed by a mixed-up story using biblical characters, places, and quotations.
    ISBN 1-57748-838-5/Paperback/224 pages/$2.97

My Final Answer by Paul Kent
Thirty separate quizzes feature twelve multiple-choice questions each—and the questions get progressively harder!
    ISBN 1-58660-030-3/Paperback/256 pages/$2.97

Bible IQ by Rayburn Ray
One hundred sections of ten questions each—and a systematic scoring system to tell you just how well you did.
    ISBN 1-57748-837-7/Paperback/256 pages/$2.97

Test Your Bible Knowledge by Carl Shoup
Over 1,400 multiple-choice questions to test your mettle, tickle your funny bone, and tantalize your intellect.
    ISBN 1-55748-541-0/Paperback/224 pages/$2.97

Fun Facts About the Bible by Robyn Martins
Challenging and intriguing Bible trivia—expect some of the answers to surprise you!
    ISBN 1-55748-897-5/Paperback/256 pages/$2.97

Available wherever books are sold.
Or order from:

Barbour Publishing, Inc.
P.O. Box 719
Uhrichsville, OH 44683
http://www.barbourbooks.com

If you order by mail add $2.00 to your order for shipping.
Prices subject to change without notice.